# FIFTY
# CIVIL WAR DOCUMENTS

D0747146

## HENRY STEELE COMMAGER

*Professor of History*
*Amherst College*

---

## AN ANVIL ORIGINAL

*under the general editorship of*

### LOUIS L. SNYDER

# ROBERT E. KRIEGER PUBLISHING COMPANY
## MALABAR, FLORIDA
### 1982

Original Edition     1965
Reprint Edition      1982

Printed and Published by
ROBERT E. KRIEGER PUBLISHING COMPANY, INC.
KRIEGER DRIVE
MALABAR, FLORIDA 32950

**Library of Congress Cataloging in Publication Data**

Main entry under title:

Fifty basic Civil War documents.

   Reprint. Originally published: Princeton, N.J.:
Van Nostrand, 1965. (An Anvil original)
   Bibliography: p.
   Includes index.
   1. United States—History—Civil War, 1861-1865—
Sources. I. Commager, Henry Steele, 1902-
[E464.F5   1982]        973.7        82-15187
ISBN 0-89874-497-0                   AACR2

# TABLE OF CONTENTS

3

# INTRODUCTION

The American Civil War has been narrated, surveyed, described, explained, analyzed, interpreted, and celebrated beyond any other period in American history, perhaps beyond any other chapter in modern history. Certainly there is no need, here, to go over ground so well-trodden, no need to interpret again the significance of the War or to justify the consideration we accord it. It is sufficient that we explain the choice of the documents we have selected and indicate their relevance to a further understanding of the War.

First, then, these readings are, with very few exceptions, documents rather than narratives, and official documents at that. The reason for this is obvious enough. Narratives are abundantly available in many existing collections—my own *The Blue and the Gray* for example. And narratives are, for the most part, far too long for reproduction in a volume of this nature. Any collection of Civil War narratives would inevitably include Haskell's wonderful account of the Battle of Gettysburg, John De Forest's story of the arduous marches through the Teche country, and General Taylor's spirited record of Stonewall Jackson's Valley Campaign; these three alone would fill all the space available to us. Second, we have resolutely excluded all military narratives and almost all documents that are primarily military. There were, altogether, over one thousand military engagements during the four years of the War; it would scarcely be illuminating to sample these—indeed, the kind of sampling we could provide would distort the military picture. Furthermore, accounts of battles, campaigns, and naval engagements, fascinating as they are, throw little light on the causes, the conduct, or the significance of the War. So these, too, have been eliminated.

The documents which we include attempt to provide a foundation and a framework for an understanding of the War. We begin, quite naturally, with the secession of the Southern states and the organization of the Confederacy, and from this we move logically to the Union response to secession—the determination to put down the rebellion and restore the Union by force. A third section presents some of the problems connected with the conduct of the War, by the North and the South—the problem of slavery, of foreign affairs, of the blockade, and of domestic politics which troubled the war years. Section four touches on some of the internal problems of the Union and the Confederacy which bore immediately on the conduct of the war—Unionism in the South, war weariness, and resentment against the Davis government; treason or near-treason in the North. Two final sections bring the story to a conclusion: one on the plans for reconstruction during the War itself, the rival plans of Lincoln and of Congressional Radicals; the other on the collapse and defeat of the Confederacy and the restoration of the Union.

It will be clear that the Union speaks more loudly and more frequently in these pages than the Confederacy. This is not merely because the Union was the larger, or because it was victorious, or because its history belongs more clearly in the mainstream of national history, or even because its literature is more voluminous. No, the explanation is more mundane than that. There are already two volumes in the Anvil series dedicated to the Confederacy: Frank Vandiver's *Basic History of the Confederacy* (Anvil No. 57) and my own volume *The Defeat of the Confederacy* (Anvil No. 71). Under the circumstances it is entirely proper that this book should reflect primarily the Union side of the War.

This is not the place to interpret the meaning of the Civil War. I have tried to do that elsewhere. It is much better to let these documents speak for themselves. Happily they can do that with complete assurance: in no other period of our history, after the Revolutionary era, were official spokesmen more thoughtful or more eloquent than during the Civil War.

Henry Steele Commager

*Amherst, Massachusetts*

# Part I

# THE SOUTH SECEDES

# — 1 —

# SOUTH CAROLINA DECLARATION OF CAUSES OF SECESSION, December 24, 1860*

*Immediately after the election of Lincoln, the legislature of South Carolina, long the leader in both the theory and the practice of nullification and secession, called a convention to meet on December 17 to consider secession. The convention, which met first at Columbia, promptly adjourned to Charleston where, on December 20, it voted unanimously for secession. Four days later it endorsed a declaration of the causes of secession, which was drafted by Christopher Memminger, who was later to be Confederate Secretary of the Treasury. Note that the South Carolina declaration of causes, like that of Mississippi, emphasizes slavery as the fundamental cause for secession.*

✓          ✓          ✓

The people of the State of South Carolina in Convention assembled, on the 2d day of April, A.D. 1852, declared that the frequent violations of the Constitution of the United States by the Federal Government, and its encroachments upon the reserved rights of the States, fully justified this State in their withdrawal from the Federal Union; but in deference to the opinions and wishes of the

* Frank Moore, ed., *The Rebellion Record* (New York, 1861), Vol. I, pp. 3 ff.

other Slaveholding States, she forbore at that time to exercise this right. Since that time these encroachments have continued to increase, and further forbearance ceases to be a virtue.

And now the State of South Carolina having resumed her separate and equal place among nations, deems it due to herself, to the remaining United States of America, and to the nations of the world, that she should declare the immediate causes which have led to this act.

In 1787, Deputies were appointed by the States to revise the articles of Confederation; and on 17th September, 1787, these Deputies recommended, for the adoption of the States, the Articles of Union, known as the Constitution of the United States.

. . . Thus was established by compact between the States, a Government with defined objects and powers, limited to the express words of the grant. . . . We hold that the Government thus established is subject to the two great principles asserted in the Declaration of Independence; and we hold further, that the mode of its formation subjects it to a third fundamental principle, namely, the law of compact. We maintain that in every compact between two or more parties, the obligation is mutual; that the failure of one of the contracting parties to perform a material part of the agreement, entirely releases the obligation of the other; and that, where no arbiter is provided, each party is remitted to his own judgment to determine the fact of failure, with all its consequences.

In the present case, that fact is established with certainty. We assert that fourteen of the States have deliberately refused for years past to fulfil their constitutional obligations, and we refer to their own statutes for the proof.

The Constitution of the United States, in its fourth Article, provides as follows:

"No person held to service or labor in one State under the laws thereof, escaping into another, shall, in consequence of any law or regulation therein, be discharged from such service or labor, but shall be delivered up, on claim of the party to whom such service or labor may be due."

This stipulation was so material to the compact that without it that compact would not have been made. The greater number of the contracting parties held slaves, and they had previously evinced their estimate of the value of such a stipulation by making it a condition in the Ordinance for the government of the territory ceded by Virginia, which obligations, and the laws of the General Government, have ceased to effect the objects of the Constitution. The States of Maine, New Hampshire, Vermont, Massachusetts, Connecticut, Rhode Island, New York, Pennsylvania, Illinois, Indiana, Michigan, Wisconsin and Iowa, have enacted laws which either nullify the acts of Congress, or render useless any attempt to execute them. In many of these States the fugitive is discharged from the service of labor claimed, and in none of them has the State Government complied with the stipulation made in the Constitution. The State of New Jersey, at an early day, passed a law in conformity with her constitutional obligation; but the current of Anti-Slavery feeling has led her more recently to enact laws which render inoperative the remedies provided by her own laws and by the laws of Congress. In the State of New York even the right of transit for a slave has been denied by her tribunals; and the States of Ohio and Iowa have refused to surrender to justice fugitives charged with murder, and with inciting servile insurrection in the State of Virginia. Thus the constitutional compact has been deliberately broken and disregarded by the non-slaveholding States; and the consequence follows that South Carolina is released from her obligation. . . .

We affirm that these ends for which this Government was instituted have been defeated, and the Government itself has been destructive of them by the action of the non-slaveholding States. Those States have assumed the right of deciding upon the propriety of our domestic institutions; and have denied the rights of property established in fifteen of the States and recognized by the Constitution; they have denounced as sinful the institution of Slavery; they have permitted the open establishment among them of societies, whose avowed object is to disturb the peace of and eloin the property of the citizens of other States. They have encouraged and assisted thousands of our slaves to leave their homes; and those who remain, have been incited by emissaries, books, and pictures, to servile insurrection.

For twenty-five years this agitation has been steadily increasing, until it has now secured to its aid the power of the common Government. Observing the *forms* of the Constitution, a sectional party has found within that article establishing the Executive Department, the means of subverting the Constitution itself. A geographical line has been drawn across the Union, and all the States north of that line have united in the election of a man to the high office of President of the United States whose opinions and purposes are hostile to Slavery. He is to be intrusted with the administration of the common Government, because he has declared that "Government cannot endure permanently half slave, half free," and that the public mind must rest in the belief that Slavery is in the course of ultimate extinction.

This sectional combination for the subversion of the Constitution has been aided, in some of the States, by elevating to citizenship persons who, by the supreme law of the land, are incapable of becoming citizens; and their votes have been used to inaugurate a new policy, hostile to the South, and destructive of its peace and safety.

On the 4th of March next this party will take possession of the Government. It has announced that the South shall be excluded from the common territory, that the Judicial tribunal shall be made sectional, and that a war must be waged against Slavery until it shall cease throughout the United States.

The guarantees of the Constitution will then no longer exist; the equal rights of the States will be lost. The Slaveholding States will no longer have the power of self-government, or self-protection, and the Federal Government will have become their enemy.

Sectional interest and animosity will deepen the irritation; and all hope of remedy is rendered vain, by the fact that the public opinion at the North has invested a great political error with the sanctions of a more erroneous religious belief.

We, therefore, the people of South Carolina, by our delegates in Convention assembled, appealing to the Supreme Judge of the world for the rectitude of our intentions, have solemnly declared that the Union heretofore existing between this State and the other States of North America is dissolved, and that the State of South Carolina has resumed her position among the nations of the world, as a separate and independent state, with full power to levy war, conclude peace, contract alliances, establish commerce, and to do all other acts and things which independent States may of right do.

## — 2 —

# Henry Timrod: "A NATION AMONG NATIONS," February 1861 *

*More than any other poet, Henry Timrod deserves the title Poet Laureate of the Confederacy. Although as a young man he had studied law in the office of that ardent Unionist James Louis Petigru and although as late as 1860 his first book of poems had been published in Boston, Timrod himself was passionately devoted to his state and his section and welcomed secession with enthusiasm.*

*"Ethnogenesis," written during the Montgomery Convention, boasted exultantly that "at last we are a nation among nations." Poor Timrod, not content with his literary contributions to the Confederacy, enlisted briefly in the Confederate Army, but poor health soon forced his withdrawal. Ill health and poverty continued to afflict him and he died two years after the War, but not before completing a melancholy companion piece to "Ethnogenesis," the Magnolia Cemetery "Ode."*

✔         ✔         ✔

*Ethnogenesis*
                                    Henry Timrod
I.

Hath not the morning dawned with added light?
And shall not evening call another star
Out of the infinite regions of the night,
To mark this day in Heaven? At last, we are

* Henry Timrod, "Ethnogenesis," in *The Poems of Henry Timrod,* Paul H. Hayne ed. (New York, 1873), pp. 100-104.

A nation among nations; and the world
Shall soon behold in many a distant port
     Another flag unfurled!
Now, come what may, whose favor need we court?
And, under God, whose thunder need we fear?
     Thank Him who placed us here
Beneath so kind a sky—the very sun
Takes part with us; and on our errands run
All breezes of the ocean; dew and rain
Do noiseless battle for us; and the Year,
And all the gentle daughters in her train,
March in our ranks, and in our service wield
     Long spears of golden grain!
A yellow blossom as her fairy shield,
June flings her azure banner to the wind,
    While in the order of their birth
Her sisters pass, and many an ample field
Grows white beneath their steps, till now, behold,
    Its endless sheets unfold
The snow of southern summers! let the earth
Rejoice! beneath those fleeces soft and warm
     Our happy land shall sleep
     In a repose as deep
As if we lay intrenched behind
Whole leagues of Russian ice and Arctic storm!

## IV.

But let our fears—if fears we have—be still,
And turn us to the future! Could we climb
Some mighty Alp, and view the coming time,
    The rapturous sight would fill
     Our eyes with happy tears!
Not only for the glories which the years
Shall bring us; not for lands from sea to sea,
And wealth, and power, and peace, though these shall be;
But for the distant peoples we shall bless,
And the hushed murmurs of a world's distress:
For, to give labor to the poor,
     The whole sad planet o'er,
And save from want and crime the humblest door,
Is one among the many ends for which
     God makes us great and rich!
The hour perchance is not yet wholly ripe
When all shall own it, but the type

Whereby we shall be known in every land
Is that vast gulf which lips our Southern strand,
And through the cold, untempered ocean pours
Its genial streams, that far off Arctic shores
May sometimes catch upon the softened breeze
Strange tropic warmth and hints of summer seas.

— 3 —

# Oliver Wendell Holmes: "BROTHER JONATHAN'S LAMENT FOR SISTER CAROLINE," 1861 *

*That amiable "autocrat" Oliver Wendell Holmes had not, like his fellow poets of New England—Lowell, Longfellow, Whittier—involved himself in the abolitionist crusade. Closer to the Brahmins—a term which he himself coined—than to the Transcendentalists, Holmes was nevertheless an ardent patriot and an ardent Unionist and, he was too, it is not to be forgotten, the father of that Captain Oliver Wendell Holmes who was later to write nationalist doctrines into the Constitution.*

*This gracious appeal to Sister Caroline was published in the* Atlantic Monthly *in 1861.*

↗          ↗          ↗

She has gone,—she has left us in passion and pride,—
Our stormy-browed sister, so long at our side!
She has torn her own star from our firmament's glow,
And turned on her brother the face of a foe!

O Caroline, Caroline, child of the sun,
We can never forget that our hearts have been one,—
Our foreheads both sprinkled in Liberty's name,
From the fountain of blood with the finger of flame!

* Oliver Wendell Holmes, *Poems* (Boston, 1862).

You were always too ready to fire at a touch;
But we said, "She is hasty,—she does not mean much."
We have scowled, when you uttered some turbulent threat;
But Friendship still whispered, "Forgive and forget!"

Has our love all died out? Have its altars grown cold?
Has the curse come at last which the fathers foretold?
Then Nature must reach us the strength of the chain
That her petulant children would sever in vain.

They may fight till the buzzards are gorged with their
      spoil,
Till the harvest grows black as it rots in the soil,
Till the wolves and the catamounts troop from their caves,
And the shark tracks the pirate, the lord of the waves.

In vain is the strife! When its fury is past,
Their fortunes must flow in one channel at last,
As the torrents that rush from the mountains of snow
Roll mingled in peace through the valleys below.

Our Union is river, lake, ocean and sky:
Man breaks not the medal, when God cuts the die!
Though darkened with sulphur, though cloven with steel,
The blue arch will brighten, the waters will heal!

O Caroline, Caroline, child of the sun,
There are battles with Fate that can never be won!
The star-flowering banner must never be furled,
For its blossoms of light are the hope of the world!

Go, then, our rash sister! afar and aloof,
Run wild in the sunshine away from our roof;
But when your heart aches and your feet have grown sore,
Remember the pathway that leads to our door!

# — 4 —

# Alexander Stephens: SLAVERY THE CORNERSTONE OF THE CONFEDERACY, March 21, 1861 *

*The diminutive Alexander Stephens of Georgia had long managed to be both a Unionist and a Southern patriot. It was to Stephens that Lincoln had written shortly after his election that there was no cause to fear "that a Republican administration would directly, or indirectly, interfere with their slaves or with them about their slaves." A delegate to the Georgia secession convention, Stephens had opposed immediate secession but had declared at the same time that, if the state seceded, he would go with the state. The Montgomery Convention named Stephens Vice-President of the Confederacy—a position for which he proved singularly ill-fitted. The "Cornerstone Speech," probably his most important political statement, was delivered at Savannah, Georgia, shortly after the organization of the Confederacy. Like so many of the declarations and resolutions of the Southerners of that day, it too emphasized slavery as the fundamental cause of the War and as the fundamental principle of the Confederacy.*

✓          ✓          ✓

. . . The new Constitution has put at rest *forever* all the agitating questions relating to our peculiar institutions —African slavery as it exists among us—the proper *status* of the negro in our form of civilization. *This was the immediate cause of the late rupture and present revolution.* JEFFERSON, in his forecast, had anticipated this, as the "rock upon which the old Union would split." He was right. What was conjecture with him, is now a realized

* Frank Moore, ed., *The Rebellion Record* (New York, 1861), Vol. I, pp. 45-46.

fact. But whether he fully comprehended the great truth upon which that rock *stood* and *stands,* may be doubted. *The prevailing ideas entertained by him and most of the leading statesmen at the time of the formation of the old Constitution were, that the enslavement of the African was in violation of the laws of nature; that it was wrong in principle, socially, morally and politically.* It was an evil they knew not well how to deal with; but the general opinion of the men of that day was that, somehow or other, in the order of Providence, the institution would be evanescent and pass away. This idea, though not incorporated in the Constitution, was the prevailing idea at the time. The Constitution, it is true, secured every essential guarantee to the institution while it should last, and hence no argument can be justly used against the constitutional guarantees thus secured, because of the common sentiment of the day. *Those ideas, however, were fundamentally wrong. They vested upon the assumption of the equality of races. This was an error.* It was a sandy foundation, and the idea of a Government built upon it—when the "storm came and the wind blew, it *fell.*"

*Our new Government is founded upon exactly the opposite ideas; its foundations are laid, its cornerstone rests, upon the great truth that the negro is not equal to the white man; that slavery, subordination to the superior race, is his natural and moral condition. This, our new Goverment, is the first, in the history of the world, based upon this great physical, philosophical, and moral truth. . . .*

. . . As I have stated, the truth of this principle may be slow in development, as all truths are, and ever have been, in the various branches of science. It was so with the principles announced by Galileo—it was so with Adam Smith and his principles of political economy. It was so with Harvey, and his theory of the circulation of the blood. It is stated that not a single one of the medical profession, living at the time of the announcement of the truths made by him, admitted them. Now, they are universally acknowledged. May we not therefore look with confidence to the ultimate universal acknowledgment of the truths upon which our system rests? It is the first Government ever instituted upon principles in strict conformity to nature, and the ordination of Providence, in furnishing the materials of human society. Many Governments have been founded upon the principles of certain classes; but the classes thus enslaved, were of the same race, and in violation of the laws of nature. Our system commits no such violation of nature's laws. The negro by nature, or by the curse against Canaan, is fitted for that condition which he occupies in our system. The architect, in the construction of buildings, lays the foundation with the proper material—the granite—then comes the brick or the marble. The substratum of our society is made of the material fitted by nature for it, and by experience we know that it is the best, not only for the superior but for the inferior race, that it should be so. It is, indeed, in conformity with the Creator. *It is not for us to inquire into the wisdom of His ordinances or to question them.* For His own purposes He has made one race to differ from another, as He has made "one star to differ from another in glory."

The great objects of humanity are best attained, when conformed to his laws and degrees, in the formation of Governments as well as in all things else. Our Confederacy is founded upon principles in strict conformity with these laws. This stone which was rejected by the first builders *"is become the chief stone of the corner"* in our new edifice. . . .

— 5 —

# THE SURRENDER OF FORT SUMTER, April 14, 1861 *

*When South Carolina seceded, Major Robert Anderson, commanding the Federal forces in Charleston, secretly moved his garrison from Fort Moultrie to Fort Sumter. The question whether his forces should be withdrawn or supported created agitation in the closing weeks of the*

* Frank Moore, ed., *The Rebellion Record* (New York, 1861), Vol. I, pp. 51-52, 76.

*Buchanan administration and the opening weeks of the Lincoln administration. While the fate of Fort Sumter was being discussed, the Confederacy took over all but four of the forts, arsenals, and military posts in the South. Against the advice of some members of his Cabinet, Lincoln finally decided not to reinforce but to provision the fort; this decision precipitated the crisis and the War. On April 11, General Beauregard, commanding the Confederate forces, demanded the immediate surrender of Fort Sumter. Major Anderson, while refusing immediate surrender, assured the Confederate emissary, Colonel Chesnut, that the fort's supplies were almost exhausted and that he would in all probability be forced to evacuate by the fifteenth. Colonel Chesnut and—we may assume—General Beauregard regarded this reply as unsatisfactory, and at dawn of April 12 the Confederate batteries opened fire on Fort Sumter.*

✔        ✔        ✔

The following is the correspondence immediately preceding the hostilities:

CHARLESTON, April 8.

L. P. WALKER, Secretary of War:

An authorized messenger from President Lincoln, just informed Gov. Pickens and myself that provisions will be sent to Fort Sumter peaceably, or otherwise by force.

G. T. BEAUREGARD.

MONTGOMERY, 10th.

Gen. G. T. BEAUREGARD, Charleston:

If you have no doubt of the authorized character of the agent who communicated to you the intention of the Washington Government, to supply Fort Sumter by force, you will at once demand its evacuation, and if this is refused, proceed in such a manner as you may determine, to reduce it. Answer.

L. P. WALKER, Sec. of War.

CHARLESTON, April 10.

L. P. WALKER, Secretary of War:

The demand will be made to-morrow at 12 o'clock

G. T. BEAUREGARD.

MONTGOMERY, April 10.

Gen. BEAUREGARD, Charleston:

Unless there are especial reasons connected with your

own condition, it is considered proper that you should make the demand at an early hour.

L. P. WALKER, Sec. of War.

CHARLESTON, April 10.
L. P. WALKER, Secretary of War, Montgomery:
The reasons are special for 12 o'clock.

G. T. BEAUREGARD.

HEADQUARTERS, PROVISIONAL ARMY, C. S. A.⎫
CHARLESTON, S. C., April 11, 1861—2 P. M.⎭

SIR: The Government of the Confederate States has hitherto forborne from any hostile demonstration against Fort Sumter, in the hope that the Government of the United States, with a view to the amicable adjustment of all questions between the two Governments, and to avert the calamities of war, would voluntarily evacuate it. There was reason at one time to believe that such would be the course pursued by the Government of the United States; and under that impression my Government has refrained from making any demand for the surrender of the fort.

But the Confederate States can no longer delay assuming actual possession of a fortification commanding the entrance of one of their harbors, and necessary to its defence and security.

I am ordered by the Government of the Confederate States to demand the evacuation of Fort Sumter. My Aids, Colonel Chesnut and Captain Lee, are authorized to make such demand of you. All proper facilities will be afforded for the removal of yourself and command, together with company, arms, and property, and all private property, to any post in the United States which you may elect. The flag which you have upheld so long and with so much fortitude, under the most trying circumstances, may be saluted by you on taking it down.

Colonel Chesnut and Captain Lee will, for a reasonable time, await your answer.

I am, sir, very respectfully,
Your obedient servant,
G. T. BEAUREGARD,
Brigadier-General Commanding.

HEADQUARTERS, FORT SUMTER, S. C.}
April 11th, 1861.

GENERAL: I have the honor to acknowledge the receipt of your communication demanding the evacuation of this fort; and to say in reply thereto that it is a demand with which I regret that my sense of honor and of my obligations to my Government prevent my compliance.

Thanking you for the fair, manly, and courteous terms proposed, and for the high compliment paid me,

I am, General, very respectfully,
Your obedient servant,
ROBERT ANDERSON,
Major U. S. Army, Commanding.

MONTGOMERY, April 11.

Gen. BEAUREGARD, Charleston:

We do not desire needlessly to bombard Fort Sumter, if Major ANDERSON will state the time at which, as indicated by him, he will evacuate, and agree that, in the mean time, he will not use his guns against us, unless ours should be employed against Fort Sumter. You are thus to avoid the effusion of blood. If this or its equivalent be refused, reduce the fort as your judgment decides to be most practicable.

L. P. WALKER, Sec. of War.

HEADQUARTERS, PROVISIONAL ARMY, C. S. A.}
CHARLESTON, April 11, 1861—11 P.M.

MAJOR: In consequence of the verbal observations made by you to my Aids, Messrs. Chesnut and Lee, in relation to the condition of your supplies, and that you would in a few days be starved out if our guns did not batter you to pieces—or words to that effect;—and desiring no useless effusion of blood, I communicated both the verbal observation and your written answer to my communication to my Government.

If you will state the time at which you will evacuate Fort Sumter, and agree that in the mean time you will not use your guns against us, unless ours shall be employed against Fort Sumter, we will abstain from opening fire upon you. Colonel Chesnut and Captain Lee are authorized by me to enter into such an agreement with you. You are therefore requested to communicate to them an open answer.

I remain, Major, very respectfully,
Your obedient servant,
G. T. BEAUREGARD,

To Brigadier-General G. T. BEAUREGARD,

HEADQUARTERS, FORT SUMTER, S. C. }
2.30 A.M., April 12, 1861.

GENERAL: I have the honor to acknowledge the receipt of your second communication of the 11th inst., by Col. Chesnut, and to state, in reply, that cordially uniting with you in the desire to avoid the useless effusion of blood, I will, if provided with the proper and necessary means of transportation, evacuate Fort Sumter by noon on the 15th instant, should I not receive, prior to that time, controlling instructions from my Government, or additional supplies; and that I will not, in the mean time, open my fire upon your forces, unless compelled to do so by some hostile act against this fort, or the flag of my Government by the forces under your command, or by some portion of them, or by the perpetration of some act showing a hostile intention on your part against this fort, or the flag it bears.

I have the honor to be, General,
Your obedient servant,
ROBERT ANDERSON,
Major U. S. A. Commanding.

Major ROBERT ANDERSON, United States Army, Commanding Fort Sumter.

FORT SUMTER, S. C. }
April 12, 1861, 3.20 A.M.

SIR: By authority of Brigadier-General Beauregard, commanding the Provisional Forces of the Confederate States, we have the honor to notify you that he will open the fire of his batteries on Fort Sumter in one hour from this time.

We have the honor to be, very respectfully,
Your obedient servants,
JAMES CHESNUT, jr.
Aide-de-Camp.
STEPHEN D. LEE,
Captain S. C. Army and Aide-de-Camp.

STEAMSHIP *Baltic*,
Off SANDY HOOK, April 18, 1861

Hon. S. CAMERON, Secretary of War, Washington, D. C.—

SIR: Having defended Fort Sumter for thirty-four hours, until the quarters were entirely burned, the main gates destroyed by fire, the gorge wall seriously injured, the magazine surrounded by flames, and its door closed from the effects of the heat, four barrels and three cartridges of powder only being available, and no provisions but pork remaining, I accepted terms of evacuation, offered by General Beauregard, being the same offered by him on the 11th inst., prior to the commencement of hostilities, and marched out of the fort Sunday afternoon, the 14th inst., with colors flying and drums beating, bringing away company and private property, and saluting my flag with fifty guns.

ROBERT ANDERSON,
Major First Artillery

## 6 —

# ROBERT E. LEE GOES
# WITH HIS STATE, 1861 *

*Robert E. Lee's decision that he could not raise his hand against his own people proved one of the most momentous of the war. No officer in the United States Army had a more brilliant record or a more distinguished career than Lee when, at the age of 54, he resigned from the Army to go with his state. He had performed brilliantly a number of difficult engineering assignments, fought gallantly in the Mexican War, served as Superintendent of the West Point Military Academy, and dealt*

* A. L. Long, *Memoirs of Robert E. Lee* (New York, 1886); Robert E. Lee, Jr., *Recollections and Letters of General Robert E. Lee* (New York, 1904), pp. 24-26.

*effectively with Indian outbreaks along the Mexican border. He was recalled to Washington early in 1861 and informally offered command of the field forces of the United States. With deep spiritual anguish he refused this offer, resigned his commission, and accepted instead command of the military forces of Virginia. Shortly after, he was appointed general in the Confederate Army and on June 1, 1862, made Commander in Chief of the Army of Northern Virginia.*

✓          ✓          ✓

## A. Col. Robert E. Lee to His Son

FORT MASON, TEXAS, January 23, 1861

The South, in my opinion, has been aggrieved by the acts of the north. . . . I feel the aggression, and am willing to take every proper step for redress. It is the principle I contend for, not individual or private benefit. As an American citizen I take great pride in my country, her prosperity, and her institutions, and would defend any state if her rights were invaded. But I can anticipate no greater calamity for the country than a dissolution of the Union. It would be an accumulation of all the evils we complain of, and I am willing to sacrifice everything but honor for its preservation. I hope, therefore, that all Constitutional means will be exhausted before there is a resort to force. Secession is nothing but revolution. The framers of our Constitution never exhausted so much labor, wisdom, and forbearance in its formation, and surrounded it with so many guards and securities, if it was intended to be broken by every member of the Confederacy at will. It is intended for "perpetual union," so expressed in the preamble, and for the establishment of a Government, not a compact, which can only be dissolved by revolution or the consent of all the people in convention assembled. It is idle to talk of secession. Anarchy would have been established, and not a Government, by Washington, Hamilton, Jefferson, Madison, and all the other patriots of the Revolution. . . . Still, a Union that can only be maintained by swords and bayonets, and in which strife and civil war are to take the place of brotherly love and kindness, has no charm for me. I shall mourn for my country and for the welfare and progress of mankind. If the Union is dissolved and the Government disrupted, I shall return to my native state and share the miseries of my people, and save in defence will draw my sword on none.

## B. To His Sister, Mrs. Anne Marshall

ARLINGTON, VIRGINIA, April 20, 1861

*My dear Sister:* I am grieved at my inability to see you. . . . I have been waiting for a 'more convenient season,' which has brought to many before me deep and lasting regret. Now we are in a state of war which will yield to nothing. The whole South is in a state of revolution, into which Virginia, after a long struggle, has been drawn; and though I recognize no necessity for this state of things, and would have forborne and pleaded to the end for redress of grievances, real or supposed, yet in my own person I had to meet the question whether I should take part against my native State.

With all my devotion to the Union and the feeling of loyalty and duty of an American citizen, I have not been able to make up my mind to raise my hand against my relatives, my children, my home. I have therefore resigned my commission in the Army, and save in defense of my native State, with the sincere hope that my poor services may never be needed, I hope I may never be called on to draw my sword. I know you will blame me; but you must think as kindly of me as you can, and believe that I have endeavoured to do what I thought right.

To show you the feeling and struggle it has cost me, I send you a copy of my letter of resignation. I have no time for more. May God guard and protect you and yours, and shower upon you everlasting blessings, is the prayer of your devoted brother,

R. E. LEE

## C. To General Scott

ARLINGTON, VIRGINIA, April 20, 1861

*General:* Since my interview with you on the 18th inst. I have felt that I ought no longer to retain my commission in the Army. I therefore tender my resignation, which I request you will recommend for acceptance. It would have been presented at once but for the struggle it has cost me to separate myself from a service to which I have devoted the best years of my life, and all the ability I possessed.

During the whole of that time—more than a quarter

of a century—I have experienced nothing but kindness from my superiors and a most cordial friendship from my comrades. To no one, General, have I been as much indebted as to yourself for uniform kindness and consideration, and it has always been my ardent desire to merit your approbation. I shall carry to the grave the most grateful recollections of your kind consideration, and your name and fame shall always be dear to me.

Save in defense of my native State, I never desire again to draw my sword.

Be pleased to accept my most earnest wishes for the continuance of your happiness and prosperity, and believe me, most truly yours,

R. E. LEE

— 7 —

# SAM HOUSTON REFUSES TO GO WITH HIS STATE, March 16, 1861 *

*Like Lee, Sam Houston had given much of his life to the service of the United States; like Lee, too, his roots were very deep in the soil of his state. Born during Washington's administration, Sam Houston had served under Andrew Jackson in the War of 1812. In 1832, Jackson sent him to Texas to negotiate a treaty with the Indians, and Houston threw in his lot with that territory, which he was soon to make an independent republic. Commander in Chief of the victorious Texan Army, he was elected the first President of the Republic of Texas; when Texas was admitted to the Union, he was its first Senator. Elec-*

---

\* "To the People of Texas," March 16, 1861, in *Writings of Sam Houston,* Amelia W. Williams and Eugene C. Barker, eds. (Austin: University of Texas Press, 1943), Vol. VIII, pp. 272-278.

*ted Governor of Texas in 1859, the aged Houston refused
to go along with or to recognize secession. Two days after
this proclamation, Houston was deposed as Governor.*

✦        ✦        ✦

FELLOW-CITIZENS: When on account of the election of
Mr. Lincoln to the Presidency of the United States, I was
urged to call the Legislature, I refused to do so until such
time as I believed the public interests required it. To all I
said, that if the people desired the Legislature to be called,
I would not stand in their way. When satisfied that the
necessity existed, I called it together, and upon the assem-
bling urged upon it the importance of immediate action in
reference to your relations with the United States and with
respect to the Frontier and the Treasury.

In the meantime, the Convention had been called,
which assembled on the 28th of January. That Convention, besides being revolutionary in its character, did not
receive the sanction of a majority of the people. As the
representative of a minority, however large, it could not
claim the right to speak for the people. It was without the
pale of the Constitution, and was unknown to the laws
which I had sworn to support. While sworn to support
the Constitution, it was my duty to stand aloof from all
revolutionary schemes calculated to subvert the Constitution. The people who were free from such solemn
obligations, might revolutionize and absolve me from
mine, my oath only having reference to my acts in the
capacity of their Chief Executive; but as a sworn officer,
my duty was too plain to be misunderstood. Because
others more lightly regarded the bond they made with
Heaven, furnished me no excuse, if my conscience con-
demned the act. If I had believed that the time had come
for revolution, I should have thrown off the burden of
an official oath, resigned my office, and as one of the
people, a free and independent citizen, have aided to
arouse my countrymen to action. I believed that the Constitution and laws would provide a remedy and therefore
I was not ready for revolution. . . .

The Legislature refused to submit the question of our
relations with the United States Government to a direct
vote of the people; but authorized the Convention to do
so. The Legislature having recognized the Convention so
far, I was willing to sanction the act, because I saw that

in no other way would the people get an opportunity to express their will. I did so, protesting against the assumption of any other powers on the part of the Convention. I knew full well the designs of the leaders of that movement. I saw that in their hands, neither Constitution or Laws would be sacred; and I put upon record my refusal to sanction any attempt on their part, to touch the charter of your liberties or infringe upon the rights secured to you by men who framed the State Constitution. . . .

This Convention has deprived the people of a right to know its doing by holding its sessions in secret. It has appointed military officers and agents under its assumed authority. It has declared by ordinance, that the people of Texas ratify the Constitution of the Provisional Government of the Confederate States, and has changed the State Constitution and established a TEST OATH of allegiance to the Confederate States, requiring all persons now in office to take the same, or suffer the penalty of removal from office; and actuated by a spirit of petty tyranny, has required the Executive and a portion of the other officers at the seat of Government to appear at its bar at a certain hour and take the same. Is has assumed to create organic laws and to put the same in execution. It has overthrown the theory of free government, by combining in itself all the Departments of Government, and exercising the powers belonging to each. Our fathers have taught us that freedom requires that these powers shall not be all lodged in, and exercised by any one body. Whenever it is so, the people suffer under a despotism.

Fellow-Citizens, I have refused to recognize this Convention. I believe that it has derived none of the powers which it has assumed either from the people or from the Legislature. I believe it guilty of an usurpation, which the people cannot suffer tamely and preserve their liberties. I am ready to lay down my life to maintain the rights and liberties of the people of Texas. I am ready to lay down the office rather than yield to usurpation and degradation.

I have declared my determination to stand by Texas in whatever position she assumes. Her people have declared in favor of a separation from the Union. I have followed her banners before, when an exile from the land of my fathers. I went back into the Union with the people of Texas. I go out from the Union with them; and though I see only gloom before me, I shall follow the "Lone Star" with the same devotion as of yore. . . .

You have withdrawn Texas from her connection with the United States. Your act changes the character of the obligation I assumed at the time of my inauguration. As Your Chief Executive, I am no longer bound to support the Constitution of the United States. . . .

I love Texas too well to bring civil strife and bloodshed upon her. To avert this calamity, I shall make no endeavor to maintain my authority as Chief Executive of this State, except by the peaceful exercise of my functions. When I can no longer do this, I shall calmly withdraw from the scene, leaving the Government in the hands of those who have usurped its authority; but still claiming that I am its Chief Executive. . . .

I PROTEST IN THE NAME OF THE PEOPLE OF TEXAS AGAINST ALL THE ACTS AND DOINGS OF THIS CONVENTION, AND I DECLARE THEM NULL AND VOID! I solemnly protest against the act of its members who are bound by no oath themselves, in declaring my office vacant, because I refuse to appear before it and take the oath prescribed.

SAM HOUSTON.

— 8 —

## Jefferson Davis: INAUGURAL ADDRESS, February 22, 1862*

*Elected provisional President of the Confederacy by the Montgomery Convention, Jefferson Davis was formally installed on February 18, 1861. At the regular presidential election, held in October, 1861, Davis was chosen for a term of six years; the date of the inaugural was deliberately set on Washington's birthday. As President,*

* Richardson, ed., *Messages and Papers of the Confederacy*, Vol. I, pp. 183 ff.

*Davis compares poorly with Lincoln, but in all likelihood he was the best possible choice for what proved to be an impossible position.*

✔        ✔        ✔

FELLOW-CITIZENS: On this the birthday of the man most identified with the establishment of American Independence, and beneath the monument erected to commemorate his heroic virtues and those of his compatriots, we have assembled to usher into existence the permanent government of the confederate States. Through this instrumentality, under the favor of Divine Providence, we hope to perpetuate the principles of our Revolutionary fathers. The day, the memory and the purpose seem fitly associated. . . .

When a long course of class legislation, directed not to the general welfare, but to the aggrandizement of the Northern section of the Union, culminated in a warfare on the domestic institutions of the Southern States—when the dogmas of a sectional party, substituted for the provisions of the constitutional compact, threatened to destroy the sovereign rights of the States, six of those States, withdrawing from the Union, confederated together to exercise the right and perform the duty of instituting a government which would better secure the liberties for the preservation of which that Union was established. . . .

For proof of the sincerity of our purpose to maintain our ancient institutions, we may point to the constitution of the Confederacy and the laws enacted under it, as well as to the fact that through all the necessities of an unequal struggle there has been no act on our part to impair personal liberty or the freedom of speech, of thought or of the press. The courts have been open, the judicial functions fully executed, and every right of the peaceful citizen maintained as securely as if a war of invasion had not disturbed the land.

The people of the States now confederated became convinced that the Government of the United States had fallen into the hands of a sectional majority, who would pervert that most sacred of all trusts to the destruction of the rights which it was pledged to protect. They believed that to remain longer in the Union would subject them to a continuance of a disparaging discrimination, submission to which would be inconsistent with their welfare, and intolerable to a proud people. They therefore determined to sever its bonds and establish a new confederacy for themselves.

The experiment instituted by our Revolutionary fathers, of a voluntary union of sovereign States for purposes specified in a solemn compact, had been perverted by those who, feeling power and forgetting right, were determined to respect no law but their own will. The Government had ceased to answer the ends for which it was ordained and established. To save ourselves from a revolution which, in its silent but rapid progress, was about to place us under the despotism of numbers, and to preserve in spirit, as well as in form, a system of government we believed to be peculiarly fitted to our condition, and full of promise for mankind, we determined to make a new association, composed of States homogeneous in interest, in policy and in feeling.

True to our traditions of peace and our love of justice, we sent commissioners to the United States to propose a fair and amicable settlement of all questions of public debt or property which might be in dispute. But the Government at Washington, denying our right to self-government, refused even to listen to any proposals for a peaceful separation. Nothing was then left to us but to prepare for war.

The first year in our history has been the most eventful in the annals of this continent. A new government has been established, and its machinery put in operation over an area exceeding seven hundred thousand square miles. The great principles upon which we have been willing to hazard everything that is dear to man have made conquests for us which could never have been achieved by the sword. Our Confederacy has grown from six to thirteen States; and Maryland, already united to us by hallowed memories and material interests, will, I believe, when able to speak with unstifled voice, connect her destiny with the South. . . .

It was, perhaps, in the ordination of Providence, that we were to be taught the value of our liberties by the price which we pay for them.

The recollections of this great contest, with all its common traditions of glory, of sacrifice and of blood, will be the bond of harmony and enduring affection amongst the people; producing unity in policy, fraternity in sentiment, and joint effort in war.

Nor have the material sacrifices of the past year been made without some corresponding benefits. If the acquiescence of foreign nations in a pretended blockade has deprived us of our commerce with them, it is fast making us a self-supporting and an independent people. The blockade, if effectual and permanent, could only serve to divert our industry from the production of articles for export, and employ it in supplying commodities for domestic use.

Fellow-citizens, after the struggles of ages had consecrated the right of the Englishman to constitutional representative government, our colonial ancestors were forced to vindicate that birthright by an appeal to arms. Success crowned their efforts, and they provided for their posterity a peaceful remedy against future aggression.

The tyranny of an unbridled majority the most odious and least responsible form of despotism, has denied us both the right and remedy. Therefore we are in arms to renew such sacrifices as our fathers made to the holy cause of constitutional liberty. At the darkest hour of our struggle the provisional gives place to the permanent government. After a series of successes and victories, which covered our arms with glory, we have recently met with serious disasters. But in the heart of a people resolved to be free, these disasters tend but to stimulate to increased resistance.

To show ourselves worthy of the inheritance bequeathed to us by the patriots of the Revolution, we must emulate that heroic devotion which made reverse to them but the crucible in which their patriotism was refined.

With confidence in the wisdom and virtue of those who will share with me the responsibility, and aid me in the conduct of public affairs; securely relying on the patriotism and courage of the people, of which the present war has furnished so many examples, I deeply feel the weight of the responsibilities I now, with unaffected diffidence, am about to assume; and, fully realizing the inequality of human power to guide and to sustain, my hope is reverently fixed on Him whose favor is ever vouchsafed to the cause which is just. With humble gratitude and adoration,

acknowledging the Providence which has so visibly protected the Confederacy during its brief but eventful career,
to Thee, O God! I trustingly commit myself, and prayer-
fully invoke thy blessing on my country and its cause.

# Part II

# "THE UNION FOREVER"

# — 9 —

# LINCOLN REFUSES TO COMPROMISE ON SLAVERY IN THE TERRITORIES,
## December, 1860 and February, 1861

*Almost immediately after the election of Lincoln, Southern extremists moved toward secession. Now that it appeared probable that the South meant what its leaders had been saying for some time and that the Union would indeed be broken up, there were frantic efforts to find some compromise which would be acceptable to both North and South. Would the North make concessions on the two crucial issues—slavery in the territories and the fugitive-slave law? Would the South accept such concessions without further assurances that the "peculiar institution" would be put beyond danger of attack? As Congressional committees and Border state committees and moderates on both sides sought desperately to find some modus vivendi, it became clear that the ultimate decision would be made by Lincoln, for the Union, and by Southern extremists, for the South. Flexible enough on most matters, Lincoln was adamant on the question of the extension of slavery in the Territories. We present here a series of letters and notes which make clear Lincoln's position. Historians are still debating the question whether a more moderate—or more acquiescent—stand by Lincoln might possibly have averted secession and war.*

✔    ✔    ✔

### A. Lincoln to Lyman Trumbull

SPRINGFIELD, ILLINOIS, December 10, 1860

My dear Sir: Let there be no compromise on the question of extending slavery. If there be, all our labor is lost, and, ere long, must be done again. The dangerous ground —that into which some of our friends have a hankering to run—is Pop. Sov. Have none of it. Stand firm. The tug has to come, and better now than any time hereafter.

### B. Lincoln to William Kellogg, M.C.*

SPRINGFIELD, ILLINOIS, December 11, 1860

Entertain no proposition for a compromise in regard to the extension of slavery. The instant you do they have us under again: all our labor is lost, and sooner or later must be done over. Douglas is sure to be again trying to bring in his "popular sovereignty." Have none of it. The tug has come, and better now than later. You know I think the fugitive-slave clause of the Constitution ought to be enforced—to put it in its mildest form, ought not to be resisted.

### C. Lincoln to E. B. Washburne†

SPRINGFIELD, ILLINOIS, December 13, 1860

My dear Sir: Yours of the 10th is received. Prevent, as far as possible, any of our friends from demoralizing themselves and our cause by entertaining propositions for compromise of any sort of "slavery extension." There is no possible compromise upon it but which puts us under again, and leaves all our work to do over again. Whether it be a Missouri line or Eli Thayer's popular sovereignty, it is all the same. Let either be done, and immediately filibustering and extending slavery recommences. On that point hold firm, as with a chain of steel.

Yours as ever,<br>A. LINCOLN

* Nicolay and Hay, eds., *The Complete Works of Abraham Lincoln,* Vol. VI, pp. 77-78.
† Nicolay and Hay, eds., *The Complete Works of Abraham Lincoln,* Vol. VI, pp. 78-79.

## D. Lincoln to Thurlow Weed *

SPRINGFIELD, ILLINOIS, December 17, 1860

My dear Sir: Yours of the 11th was received two days ago. Should the convocation of governors of which you speak seem desirous to know my views on the present aspect of things tell them you judge from my speeches that I will be inflexible on the territorial question; that I probably think either the Missouri line extended, or Douglas's and Eli Thayer's popular sovereignty, would lose us everything we gain by the election; that filibustering for all south of us and making slave States of it would follow, in spite of us, in either case; also that I probably think all opposition, real and apparent, to the fugitive-slave clause of the Constitution ought to be withdrawn. . . .

## E. Lincoln to Lyman Trumbull

SPRINGFIELD, ILLINOIS, December 21, 1860

My dear Sir: Thurlow Weed was with me nearly all day yesterday, and left last night with three short resolutions which I drew up, and which, or the substance of which, I think, would do much good if introduced and unanimously supported by our friends. They do not touch the territorial question. Mr. Weed goes to Washington with them; and says that he will first of all confer with you and Mr. Hamlin. I think it would be best for Mr. Seward to introduce them, and Mr. Weed will let him know that I think so. Show this to Mr. Hamlin, but beyond him do not let my name be known in the matter.

## F. Lincoln's "Three Propositions," December 20, 1860 †

*In the Seward manuscripts is a statement, in Lincoln's handwriting, of the three propositions that Lincoln made to Thurlow Weed at their meeting on December 20. Weed gave these to Seward, who in turn submitted them to some of the members of the "Union Saving Committee" —Doolittle, Collamer, Grimes, and Wade—as well as Fessenden and Trumbull. This group decided that the resolutions would "divide our friends" and therefore did*

* Nicolay and Hay, eds., *The Complete Works of Abraham Lincoln*, Vol. VI, p. 82.

† Frederic Bancroft, *The Life of William H. Seward* (New York, 1900), Vol. II, 10 n.

*not submit them to the Republicans in Congress. The resolutions are as follows:*

✔          ✔          ✔

Resolved:

That the fugitive-slave clause of the Constitution ought to be enforced by a law of Congress, with efficient provisions for that object, not obliging private persons to assist in its execution, but punishing all who resist it, and with the usual safeguards to liberty, securing free men against being surrendered as slaves—

That all state laws, if there be such, really, or apparently, in conflict with such law of Congress, ought to be repealed; and no opposition to the execution of such law of Congress ought to be made—

That the Federal Union must be preserved.

## G. Hon. W. H. Seward *

SPRINGFIELD, ILLINOIS, February 1, 1861

My dear Sir: On the 21st. ult. Hon. W. Kellogg, a Republican M.C. of this state, whom you probably know, was here, in a good deal of anxiety, seeking to ascertain to what extent I would be consenting for our friends to go in the way of compromise on the now vexed question. While he was with me I received a despatch from Senator Trumbull, at Washington, alluding to the same question, and telling me to await letters. I thereupon told Mr. Kellogg that when I should receive these letters, posting me as to the state of affairs at Washington, I would write you, requesting you to let him see my letter. To my surprise when the letters mentioned by Judge Trumbull came, they made no allusion to the "vexed question." This baffled me so much that I was near not writing you at all, in compliance with what I had said to Judge Kellogg.

I say now, however, as I have all the while said, that on the territorial question—that is, the question of extending slavery under the national auspices—I am inflexible. I am for no compromise which *assists* or *permits* the extension of the institution on soil owned by the nation. And any trick by which the nation is to acquire territory, and then allow some local authority to spread slavery over it, is as obnoxious as any other.

* Nicolay and Hay, eds., *The Complete Works of Lincoln,* Vol. VI, pp. 102-104.

I take it that to effect some such result as this, and to put us again on the high-road to a slave empire is the object of all these proposed compromises. I am against it.

As to fugitive slaves, District of Columbia, slave trade among the slave trades, and whatever springs of necessity from the fact that the institution is amongst us, I care but little, so that what is done be comely, and not altogether outrageous. Nor do I care much about New Mexico, if further extension were hedged against.

Yours very truly
A. LINCOLN

# — 10 —

# J. J. Crittenden: A PLEA FOR COMPROMISE, March 2, 1861*

*No statesman worked harder for the preservation of the Union or contributed more to compromise sectional differences than John J. Crittenden of Kentucky. Born in the year of the Federal Constitutional Convention, he was all his life an ardent nationalist, and it may be said that he inherited the mantle of Henry Clay. Bitterly opposed to secession, Crittenden was almost as strongly opposed to any interference in the "domestic" institutions of the States. His famous Compromise Resolutions* (see Document No. 15) *sought to commit the government to a limited war. In December, 1860, he tried in vain to pledge the Congress to an extension of the Missouri Compromise of 1820, and the following month he sought a national referendum on this and other compromise proposals. He was a member, too, of the peace convention which failed so signally to agree upon measures to avoid war; he was more successful in his efforts to keep his own state of Kentucky in the Union. It is interesting to note that one of Crittenden's sons fought in the Confederate*

* *Congressional Globe,* 36 Congress, 2 Session, pp. 1375-1380.

*Army and another in the Union Army. This "plea for peace" is taken from his final appeal to Congress just before the outbreak of the War.*

✓                    ✓                    ✓

Mr. President, it is an admitted fact that our Union, to some extent, has already been dismembered; and that further dismemberment is impending and threatened. It is a fact that the country is in danger. This is admitted on all hands. It is our duty, if we can, to provide a remedy for this. . . . Remedies have been proposed; resolutions have been offered, proposing for adoption measures which it was thought would satisfy the country. . . . We have passed none of these measures. The differences of opinion among Senators have been such that we have not been able to concur in any of the measures which have been proposed. . . . We are about to adjourn. We have done nothing. Even the Senate of the United States, beholding this great ruin around them, beholding dismemberment and revolution going on, and civil war threatened as the result, have been able to do nothing; we have done absolutely nothing. Sir, is not this a remarkable spectacle? How does it happen that not even a bare majority here, when the country trusted to our hands is going to ruin, have been competent to devise any measure of public safety? . . . We see the danger; we acknowledge our duty; and yet, with all this before us, we are acknowledging before the world that we can do nothing; acknowledging before the world, or appearing to all the world, as men who do nothing. . . .

Mr. President, the cause of this great discontent in the country, the cause of the evils which we now suffer and which we now fear, originates chiefly from questions growing out of the respective territorial rights of the different States and the unfortunate subject of slavery. . . . I do not appear on this occasion as the advocate of slavery; I appear here as the advocate of the Union. I want to preserve that from overthrow; and I am suggesting that policy, which, according to my poor judgment, is adequate to the object.

What is the great question out of which this mighty mischief has grown; what is this question about territory? Practically, it is reduced to a very small matter. We have passed through many of these territorial difficulties; we have now arrived at the very last one of them. Neither the climate nor the wishes of any portion of this Union have induced the people anywhere to desire really to extend slavery above the line of 36° 30′ north latitude. . . . We have now much territory north of that line; but there is no pretension to any rights there by those who hold slaves. We have since that compromise line was first established, acquired territory south of it. That territory south of it is composed of the Territory of New Mexico, and nothing else; and there slavery now exists by law. . . . These points of controversy have reference practically now to no other Territory which we have except the Territory of New Mexico; and to show how infinitely small that is, there is another consideration to which I wish to advert. What are the worth and value of that Territory to white or to black? It is the most sterile region of country belonging to the United States, the least happy. It has been open to slavery for ten years, and there is a controversy, I believe, whether there are twenty-four or twenty-six or twenty-eight slaves within the whole Territory. As I believe, it can never be made a slave State. . . . Here is a mere question of abstract right, in the deprivation of which the South has supposed itself to be offended. . . .

Thirty-seven thousand men from the noble old State of Massachusetts have said, "Let there be no compromise." . . .

Sir, if old Bunker Hill now had a voice, it would be, of course, as it should be, a voice like thunder; and what would she proclaim from her old and triumphant heights? No compromise with your brethren? No, sir; that would not be her voice; but I fancy to myself, if that venerated and honored old scene of American bravery, hallowed by the blood of the patriots who stood there, hand in hand, brethren of the North and South, could but speak, it would be but one voice, a great and patriotic voice: peace with thy brethren; be reconciled with thy brethren. It is less than the value of a straw that is asked from you as compromise, and you will not give a straw. You prefer the bloody doctrine of "No compromise; battle first;" and woe be to those who first draw the sword. . . .

I fear for further revolution—for revolution to such

an extent as to destroy, in effect, this Union. I hope not. I would advise against it. I would say to the people [of the South] . . . Be patient. . . . Hold fast to the Union. The Union is the instrument by which you may obtain redress, by which you will in the end obtain redress. Congress may err. It may err from error of judgment, from passion, from excitement, from party heats; they will not last always. The principles upon which your Government was founded recognize all these frailties, recognize all these sources of occasional and temporary wrong and injustice, but they furnish a remedy for it. They furnish a remedy in the often-recurring elections which the people make. It is not for the first offense that dismemberment and disunion are justified. Hold fast to the Union. There is safety, tried safety, known safety; and that same Union is the best assurance you can have of eventually obtaining from your fellow-citizens a generous recompense for all the wrongs you have received, and a generous remedy against any wrongs hereafter.

These are my feelings, and this would be my advice. My advice is that of a Union man earnest for its preservation. . . . stay in the Union and strive in the Union. . . .

Through this great nation common blood flows. What man is there here that is not of a blood, flowing—meandering—perhaps through every State in the Union? and we talk about not compromising a family quarrel; and that is to be held up as patriotism, or party fidelity. In the name of God, who is it that will adopt that policy? We are one people in blood; in language one; in thoughts one; we read the same books; we feed on the same meats; we go to the same school; we belong to the same communion. If, as we go through this quarrelsome world, we meet with our little difficulties, if we wish to carry with us grateful hearts of the blessings we have enjoyed, we shall be bound to compromise with the difficulties that must occur on all the ways of the world that are trodden by Governments on earth. It is our infirmity to have such difficulties. Let it be our magnanimity and our wisdom to compromise and settle them. . . .

My principle, and the doctrine I teach, is, take care of the Union; compromise it; do anything for it; it is the palladium—so General Washington called it—of your rights; take care of it, and it will take care of you. Yes, sir; let us take care of the Union, and it will certainly take care of us. That is the proposition which I teach.

# — 11 —

## Lincoln: FIRST INAUGURAL ADDRESS, March 4, 1861 *

*In his first inaugural address, President Lincoln restated his conviction that the Union was older than the States and that the contract between the States was binding and irrevocable. The last paragraph of the inaugural was written by Secretary Seward.*

✓        ✓        ✓

FELLOW-CITIZENS OF THE UNITED STATES:—In compliance with a custom as old as the Government itself, I appear before you to address you briefly, and to take in your presence the oath prescribed by the Constitution of the United States to be taken by the President "before he enters on the execution of his office." . . .

Apprehension seems to exist among the people of the Southern States that by the accession of a Republican administration their property and their peace and personal security are to be endangered. There has never been any reasonable cause for such apprehension. Indeed, the most ample evidence to the contrary has all the while existed and been open to their inspection. It is found in nearly all the published speeches of him who now addresses you. I do but quote from one of those speeches when I declare that "I have no purpose, directly or indirectly, to interfere with the institution of slavery in the States where it exists. I believe I have no lawful right to do so, and I have no inclination to do so." . . .

* Richardson, ed., *Messages and Papers of the Confederacy,* Vol. VI, pp. 5 ff.

I now reiterate these sentiments; and, in doing so, I only press upon the public attention the most conclusive evidence of which the case is susceptible, that the property, peace and security of no section are to be in any wise endangered by the now incoming administration. I add, too, that all the protection which, consistently with the Constitution and the laws, can be given, will be cheerfully given to all the States when lawfully demanded, for whatever cause—as cheerfully to one section as to another. . . .

I take the official oath to-day with no mental reservations, and with no purpose to construe the Constitution or laws by any hypercritical rules. And, while I do not choose now to specify particular acts of Congress as proper to be enforced, I do suggest that it will be much safer for all, both in official and private stations, to conform to and abide by all those acts which stand unrepealed, than to violate any of them, trusting to find impunity in having them held to be unconstitutional. . . .

A disruption of the Federal Union, heretofore only menaced, is now formidably attempted.

I hold that, in contemplation of universal law and of the Constitution, the Union of these States is perpetual. Perpetuity is implied, if not expressed, in the fundamental law of all national governments. It is safe to assert that no government proper ever had a provision in its organic law for its own termination. Continue to execute all the express provisions of our national Constitution, and the Union will endure forever—it being impossible to destroy it except by some action not provided for in the instrument itself.

Again, if the United States be not a government proper, but an association of States in the nature of contract merely, can it as a contract be peacefully unmade by less than all the parties who made it? One party to a contract may violate it—break it, so to speak; but does it not require all to lawfully rescind it?

Descending from these general principles, we find the proposition that in legal contemplation the Union is perpetual confirmed by the history of the Union itself. The Union is much older than the Constitution. It was formed, in fact, by the Articles of Association in 1774. It was matured and continued by the Declaration of Independence in 1776. It was further matured, and the faith of all the then thirteen States expressly plighted and engaged that it should be perpetual, by the Articles of Confederation in 1778. And, finally, in 1787 one of the declared objects for ordaining and establishing the Constitution was "to form a more perfect Union."

But if the destruction of the Union by one or by a part only of the States be lawfully possible, the Union is less perfect than before the Constitution, having lost the vital element of perpetuity.

It follows from these views that no State upon its own mere motion can lawfully get out of the Union; that resolves and ordinances to that effect are legally void; and that acts of violence, within any State or States, against the authority of the United States, are insurrectionary or revolutionary, according to circumstances.

I therefore consider that, in view of the Constitution and the laws, the Union is unbroken; and to the extent of my ability I shall take care, as the Constitution itself expressly enjoins upon me, that the laws of the Union be faithfully executed in all the States. Doing this I deem to be only a simple duty on my part; and I shall perform it so far as practicable, unless my rightful masters, the American people, shall withhold the requisite means, or in some authoritative manner direct the contrary. I trust this will not be regarded as a menace, but only as the declared purpose of the Union that it will constitutionally defend and maintain itself.

In doing this there needs to be no bloodshed or violence; and there shall be none, unless it be forced upon the national authority. The power confided to me will be used to hold, occupy, and possess the property and places belonging to the Government, and to collect the duties and imposts; but beyond what may be necessary for these objects, there will be no invasion, no using of force against or among the people anywhere. Where hostility to the United States, in any interior locality, shall be so great and universal as to prevent competent resident citizens from holding the Federal offices, there will be no attempt to force obnoxious strangers among the people for that object. While the strict legal right may exist in the government to enforce the exercise of these offices, the attempt to do so would be so irritating, and so nearly impracticable withal, that I deem it better to forego for the time the uses of such offices.

The mails, unless repelled, will continue to be furnished in all parts of the Union. So far as possible, the people everywhere shall have that sense of perfect security which is most favorable to calm thought and reflection. The course here indicated will be followed unless current events and experience shall show a modification or change to be proper, and in every case and exigency my best discretion will be exercised according to circumstances actually existing, and with a view and a hope of a peaceful solution of the national troubles and the restoration of fraternal sympathies and affections.

That there are persons in one section or another who seek to destroy the Union at all events, and are glad of any pretext to do it, I will neither affirm nor deny; but if there be such, I need address no word to them. To those, however, who really love the Union may I not speak?

Before entering upon so grave a matter as the destruction of our national fabric, with all its benefits, its memories, and its hopes, would it not be wise to ascertain precisely why we do it? Will you hazard so desperate a step while there is any possibility that any portion of the ills you fly from have no real existence? Will you, while the certain ills you fly to are greater than all the real ones you fly from—will you risk the commission of so fearful a mistake?

All profess to be content in the Union if all constitutional rights can be maintained. Is it true, then, that any right, plainly written in the Constitution, has been denied? I think not. Happily the human mind is so constituted that no party can reach to the audacity of doing this. Think, if you can, of a single instance in which a plainly written provision of the Constitution has ever been denied. If by the mere force of numbers a majority should deprive a minority of any clearly written constitutional right, it might, in a moral point of view, justify revolution—certainly would if such a right were a vital one. But such is not our case. All the vital rights of minorities and of individuals are so plainly assured to them by affirmations and negations, guaranties and prohibitions, in the Constitution, that controversies never arise concerning them. But no organic law can ever be framed with a provision specifically applicable to every question which may occur in practical administration. No foresight can anticipate, nor any document of reasonable length contain, express provisions for all possible questions. Shall fugitives from labor be surrendered by national or by State authority? The Constitution does not expressly say. *May* Congress prohibit slavery in the Territories? The Constitution does not expressly say. *Must* Congress protect slavery in the Territories? The Constitution does not expressly say.

From questions of this class spring all our constitutional controversies, and we divide upon them into majorities and minorities. If the minority will not acquiesce, the majority must, or the Government must cease. There is no other alternative; for continuing the Government is acquiescence on one side or the other.

If a minority in such case will secede rather than acquiesce, they make a precedent which in turn will divide and ruin them; for a minority of their own will secede from them whenever a majority refuses to be controlled by such minority. For instance, why may not any portion of a new confederacy a year or two hence arbitrarily secede again, precisely as portions of the present Union now claim to secede from it? All who cherish disunion sentiments are now being educated to the exact temper of doing this.

Is there such perfect identity of interests among the States to compose a new Union as to produce harmony only, and prevent renewed secession?

Plainly, the central idea of secession is the essence of anarchy. A majority held in restraint by constitutional checks and limitations, and always changing easily with deliberate changes of popular opinions and sentiments, is the only true sovereign of a free people. Whoever rejects it does, of necessity, fly to anarchy or to despotism. Unanimity is impossible; the rule of a minority, as a permanent arrangement, is wholly inadmissible; so that, rejecting the majority principle, anarchy or despotism in some form is all that is left.

I do not forget the position assumed by some, that constitutional questions are to be decided by the Supreme Court; nor do I deny that such decisions must be binding, in any case, upon the parties to a suit, as to the object of that suit, while they are also entitled to a very high respect and consideration in all parallel cases by all other departments of the government. And, while it is obviously possible that such decision may be erroneous in any given case, still the evil effect following it, being limited to that particular case, with the chance that it may be overruled and never become a precedent for other cases, can better be borne than could the evils of a different practice. At the same time, the candid citizen must confess that if the policy of the government, upon vital questions affecting the whole people, is to be irrevocably fixed by decisions of the Supreme Court, the instant they are made, in ordinary litigation between parties in personal actions, the people will have ceased to be their own rulers, having to that extent practically resigned the government into the hands of that eminent tribunal. Nor is there in this view any assault upon the court or the judges. It is a duty from which they may not shrink to decide cases properly brought before them, and it is no fault of their if others seek to turn their decisions to political purposes.

One section of our country believes slavery is right, and ought to be extended, while the other believes it is wrong, and ought not to be extended. This is the only substantial dispute. The fugitive slave clause of the Constitution and the law for the suppression of the foreign slave trade are each as well enforced, perhaps, as any law can ever be in a community where the moral sense of the people imperfectly supports the law itself. The great body of the people abide by the dry legal obligation in both cases, and a few break over in each. This, I think, cannot be perfectly cured; and it would be worse in both cases after the separation of the sections than before. The foreign slave trade, now imperfectly suppressed, would be ultimately revived, without restriction, in one section, while fugitive slaves, now only partially surrendered, would not be surrendered at all by the other.

Physically speaking, we cannot separate. We cannot remove our respective sections from each other, nor build an impassable wall between them. A husband and wife may be divorced and go out of the presence and beyond the reach of each other; but the different parts of our country cannot do this. They cannot but remain face to face, and intercourse, either amicable or hostile, must continue between them. Is it possible, then, to make that intercourse more advantageous or more satisfactory after separation than before? Can aliens make treaties easier than friends can make laws? Can treaties be more faithfully enforced between aliens than laws can among friends? Suppose you go to war, you cannot fight always;

and when, after much loss on both sides, and no gain on either, you cease fighting, the identical old questions as to terms of intercourse are again upon you.

This country, with its institutions, belongs to the people who inhabit it. Whenever they shall grow weary of the existing government, they can exercise their constitutional right of amending it, or their revolutionary right to dismember or overthrow it. I cannot be ignorant of the fact that many worthy and patriotic citizens are desirous of having the national Constitution amended. While I make no recommendation of amendments, I fully recognize the rightful authority of the people over the whole subject, to be exercised in either of the modes prescribed in the instrument itself, and I should, under existing circumstances, favor rather than oppose a fair opportunity being afforded the people to act upon it. I will venture to add that to me the convention mode seems preferable, in that it allows amendments to originate with the people themselves, instead of only permitting them to take or reject propositions originated by others not especially chosen for the purpose, and which might not be precisely such as they would wish to either accept or refuse. I understand a proposed amendment to the Constitution— which amendment, however, I have not seen—has passed Congress, to the effect that the Federal Government shall never interfere with the domestic institutions of the States, including that of persons held to service. To avoid misconstruction of what I have said, I depart from my purpose not to speak of particular amendments so far as to say that, holding such a provision to now be implied constitutional law, I have no objection to its being made express and irrevocable. . . .

Why should there not be a patient confidence in the ultimate justice of the people? Is there any better or equal hope in the world? In our present differences is either party without faith of being in the right? If the Almighty Ruler of nations, with his eternal truth and justice, be on your side of the North, or on yours of the South, that truth and that justice will surely prevail by the judgment of this great tribunal of the American people.

By the frame of the government under which we live, this same people have wisely given their public servants but little power for mischief; and have, with equal wisdom, provided for the return of that little to their own hands at very short intervals. While the people retain their virtue and vigilance, no administration, by any extreme of wickedness or folly, can very seriously injure the government in the short space of four years.

My countrymen, one and all, think calmly and well upon this whole subject. Nothing valuable can be lost by taking time. If there be an object to hurry any of you in hot haste to a step which you would never take deliberately, that object will be frustrated by taking time; but no good object can be frustrated by it. Such of you as are now dissatisfied still have the old Constitution unimpaired, and, on the sensitive point, the laws of your own framing under it; while the new administration will have no immediate power, if it would, to change either. If it were admitted that you who are dissatisfied hold the right side in the dispute, there still is no single good reason for precipitate action. Intelligence, patriotism, Christianity, and a firm reliance on Him who has never yet forsaken this favored land, are still competent to adjust in the best way all our present difficulty.

In your hands, my dissatisfied fellow-countrymen, and not in mine, is the momentous issue of civil war. The government will not assail you. You can have no conflict without being yourselves the aggressors. You have no oath registered in heaven to destroy the government, while I shall have the most solemn one to "preserve, protect, and defend" it.

I am loath to close. We are not enemies, but friends. We must not be enemies. Though passion may have strained, it must not break, our bonds of affection. The mystic chords of memory, stretching from every battlefield and patriot grave to every living heart and hearthstone all over this broad land, will yet swell the chorus of the Union when again touched, as surely they will be, by the better angels of our nature.

## — 12 —

# W. H. Seward: A PLAN TO AVERT CIVIL WAR, April 1, 1861 *

*One of the founders of the Republican Party and the most prominent of the candidates for the nomination in 1860, William H. Seward looked upon his appointment as Secretary of State as nothing more than his due. In the beginning he, like so many others, failed signally to appreciate Lincoln's talents and character and regarded him instead with condescension. "Seward" said Gideon Wells, "liked to be called premier." These "Thoughts for the President's Consideration" were intended by Seward to establish his control over the President and presidential policies. Lincoln's reply was a masterly rebuke, all the more masterly because it did not alienate Seward.*

✓          ✓          ✓

*Some Thoughts for the President's Consideration, April 1, 1861.*

*First.* We are at the end of a month's administration, and yet without a policy either domestic or foreign.

*Second.* This, however, is not culpable, and it has even been unavoidable. The presence of the Senate, with the need to meet applications for patronage, have prevented attention to other and more grave matters.

*Third.* But further delay to adopt and prosecute our policies for both domestic and foreign affairs would not only bring scandal on the administration, but danger upon the country.

*Fourth.* To do this we must dismiss the applicants for office. But how? I suggest that we make the local appoint-

* *The Writings of Abraham Lincoln,* Constitutional ed., Vol. V, pp. 278 ff.

ments forthwith, leaving foreign or general ones for ulterior and occasional action.

*Fifth.* The policy at home. I am aware that my views are singular, and perhaps not sufficiently explained. My system is built upon this idea as a ruling one, namely, that we must

CHANGE THE QUESTION BEFORE THE PUBLIC FROM ONE UPON SLAVERY, OR ABOUT SLAVERY, for a question upon UNION OR DISUNION:

In other words, from what would be regarded as a party question, to one of patriotism or union.

The occupation or evacuation of Fort Sumter, although not in fact a slavery or a party question, is so regarded. Witness the temper manifested by the Republicans in the free States, and even by the Union men in the South.

I would therefore terminate it as a safe means for changing the issue. I deem it fortunate that the last administration created the necessity.

For the rest, I would simultaneously defend and reinforce all the ports in the gulf, and have the navy recalled from foreign stations to be prepared for a blockade. Put the island of Key West under martial law.

This will raise distinctly the question of union or disunion. I would maintain every fort and possession in the South.

## FOR FOREIGN NATIONS

I would demand explanations from Spain and France, categorically, at once.

I would seek explanations from Great Britain and Russia, and send agents into Canada, Mexico, and Central America to rouse a vigorous continental spirit of independence on this continent against European intervention.

And, if satisfactory explanations are not received from Spain and France,

Would convene Congress and declare war against them.

But whatever policy we adopt, there must be an energetic prosecution of it.

For this purpose it must be somebody's business to pursue and direct it incessantly.

Either the President must do it himself, and be all the while active in it, or

Devolve it on some member of his Cabinet. Once

adopted, debates on it must end, and all agree and abide.

It is not in my especial province;

But I neither seek to evade nor assume responsibility.

### REPLY TO SECRETARY SEWARD'S MEMORANDUM

Executive Mansion, April 1, 1861.

HON. W. H. SEWARD

MY DEAR SIR:—Since parting with you I have been considering your paper dated this day, and entitled "Some Thoughts for the President's Consideration." The first proposition in it is, *"First,* We are at the end of a month's administration, and yet without a policy either domestic or foreign."

At the beginning of that month, in the inaugural, I said: "The power confided to me will be used to hold, occupy, and possess the property and places belonging to the Government and to collect the duties and imposts." This had your distinct approval at the time; and, taken in connection with the order I immediately gave General Scott, directing him to employ every means in his power to strengthen and hold the forts, comprises the exact domestic policy you now urge, with the single exception that it does not propose to abandon Fort Sumter.

Again, I do not perceive how the reinforcement of Fort Sumter would be done on a slavery or a party issue, while that of Fort Pickens would be on a more national and patriotic one.

The news received yesterday in regard to St. Domingo certainly brings a new item within the range of our foreign policy; but up to that time we have been preparing circulars and instructions to ministers and the like, all in perfect harmony, without even a suggestion that we had no foreign policy.

Upon your closing propositions—that "whatever policy we adopt, there must be an energetic prosecution of it.

"For this purpose it must be somebody's business to pursue and direct it incessantly.

"Either the President must do it himself, and be all the while active in it, or

"Devolve it on some member of his Cabinet. Once adopted, debates on it must end, and all agree and abide" —I remark that if this must be done, I must do it. When a general line of policy is adopted, I apprehend there is no danger of its being changed without good reason, or continuing to be a subject of unnecessary debate; still, upon points arising in its progress I wish, and suppose I am entitled to have, the advice of all the Cabinet.

Your obedient servant,

A. LINCOLN

# — 13 —

# PROCLAMATION OF A BLOCKADE, April 19, 1861 *

*"The blockade of the Confederacy," writes one critic, "was an undertaking without precedent in history." To bottle up a dozen major ports and about 200 minor ports along a coastline of approximately 3600 miles was indeed a formidable if not an impossible task. The Union had at the outbreak of the War less than 20 vessels, most of these antiquated, and for two years or more the blockade was largely ineffective. Then the Navy yards performed miracles of shipbuilding, and by the end of the War, the Union Navy's ships numbered over 600. In the meantime, too, the task of blockading the Confederacy had been greatly simplified by two unrelated events: one, the capture of major southern ports such as Norfolk and New Orleans and two, the failure of cotton to establish its claim to kingship sufficiently to compel Britain to break the blockade.*

✦          ✦          ✦

April 19, 1861

Whereas an insurrection against the government of the United States has broken out in the States of South Carolina, Georgia, Alabama, Florida, Mississippi, Louisiana, and Texas, and the laws of the United States for the col-

* Richardson, ed., *Messages and Papers of the Confederacy.*

lection of the revenue cannot be effectually executed therein conformably to that provision of the Constitution which requires duties to be uniform throughout the United States:

And whereas a combination of persons engaged in such insurrection have threatened to grant pretended letters of marque to authorize the bearers thereof to commit assaults on the lives, vessels, and property of good citizens of the country lawfully engaged in commerce on the high seas, and in waters of the United States. . . .

Now, therefore, I, Abraham Lincoln, President of the United States, with a view to the same purposes before mentioned, and to the protection of the public peace, and the lives and property of quiet and orderly citizens pursuing their lawful occupations, until Congress shall have assembled and deliberated on the said unlawful proceedings, or until the same shall have ceased, have further deemed it advisable to set on foot a blockade of the ports within the States aforesaid, in pursuance of the laws of the United States, and of the law of nations in such case provided. For this purpose a competent force will be posted so as to prevent entrance and exit of vessels from the ports aforesaid. If, therefore, with a view to violate such blockade, a vessel shall approach or shall attempt to leave either of the said ports, she will be duly warned by the commander of one of the blockading vessels, who will indorse on her register the fact and date of such warning, and if the same vessel shall again attempt to enter or leave the blockaded port, she will be captured and sent to the nearest convenient port, for such proceedings against her and her cargo, as prize, as may be deemed advisable.

And I hereby proclaim and declare that if any person, under the pretended authority of the said States, or under any other pretense, shall molest a vessel of the United States, or the persons or cargo on board of her, such person will be held amenable to the laws of the United States for the prevention and punishment of piracy.

# — 14 —

# THE SUPREME COURT UPHOLDS THE BLOCKADE: THE PRIZE CASES, 1863*

*Was the blockade legal? That depended on a number of considerations. Was the rebellion a war? Could the President proclaim a blockade without recognition of a state of war by the Congress? If the War was merely suppression of an insurrection, could the United States invoke what was after all an instrument of international law and expect or require other nations to respect it? Alleging that only Congress could declare war, that there had been no such declaration or even recognition of war by Congress, that a blockade is an instrument of war, and that the Presidential proclamation of the blockade was therefore illegal, a group of owners whose ships had been seized as prizes for trying to run the blockade sued for recovery of their property.*

*Justice Grier, in his decision in the so-called Prize Cases, recognized the existence of a state of war, sustained the blockade, and denounced the illegality of secession. But it was a close thing. Astonishing as it may seem today, four judges dissented.*

✓          ✓          ✓

Mr. Justice Grier: Let us inquire whether, at the time this blockade was instituted, a state of war existed which would justify a resort to these means of subduing the hostile force.

War has been well defined to be, "That state in which a nation prosecutes its right by force."

The parties belligerent in a public war are independent nations. But it is not necessary, to constitute war, that

* 67 United States Supreme Court Reports 635.

both parties should be acknowledged as independent nations or sovereign States. A war may exist where one of the belligerents claims sovereign rights as against the other.

Insurrection against a government may or may not culminate in an organized rebellion, but a civil war always begins by insurrection against the lawful authority of the government. A civil war is never solemnly declared; it becomes such by its accidents—the number, power, and organization of the persons who originate and carry it on. When the party in rebellion occupy and hold in a hostile manner a certain portion of territory; have declared their independence; have cast off their allegiance; have organized armies; have commenced hostilities against their former Sovereign, the world acknowledges them as belligerents, and the contest a war. They claim to be in arms to establish their liberty and independence, in order to become a sovereign State, while the sovereign party treats them as insurgents and rebels who owe allegiance, and who should be punished with death for their treason. . . .

As a civil war is never publicly proclaimed, *eo nomine* against insurgents, its actual existence is a fact in our domestic history which the court is bound to notice and to know. . . .

This greatest of civil wars was not gradually developed by popular commotion, tumultuous assemblies, or local unorganized insurrections. However long may have been its previous conception, it nevertheless sprung forth suddenly from the parent brain, a Minerva in the full panoply of war. The President was bound to meet it in the shape it presented itself, without waiting for Congress to baptize it with a name; and no name given to it by him or them could change the fact.

It is not the less a civil war, with belligerent parties in hostile array, because it may be called an "insurrection" by one side, and the insurgents be considered as rebels or traitors. It is not necessary that the independence of the revolted province or State be acknowledged in order to constitute it a party belligerent in a war according to the law of nations. Foreign nations acknowledge it as war by a declaration of neutrality. The condition of neutrality cannot exist unless there be two belligerent parties. . . .

After such an official recognition by the sovereign, a citizen of a foreign State is estopped to deny the existence of a war, with all its consequences, as regards neutrals. They cannot ask a court to affect a technical ignorance of the existence of a war, which all the world acknowledges to be the greatest civil war known in the history of the human race, and thus cripple the arm of the government and paralyze its power by subtile definitions and ingenious sophisms.

The law of nations is also called the law of nature; it is founded on the common consent as well as the common sense of the world. It contains no such anomalous doctrine as that which this court are now for the first time desired to pronounce, to wit: That insurgents who have risen in rebellion against their sovereign, expelled her courts, established a revolutionary government, organized armies, and commenced hostilities, are not enemies because they are traitors; and a war levied on the government by traitors, in order to dismember and destroy, it, is not a war because it is an "insurrection."

## — 15 —

# CRITTENDEN-JOHNSON RESOLUTIONS ON THE WAR, July, 1861 *

*These Resolutions represent the effort of Southern moderates and conservatives to commit the North to limited war objectives and to moderation toward slavery. Both were introduced in December, 1860. The Crittenden Resolutions passed the House, January 22, 1861, with only two dissenting votes; the Johnson Resolutions passed the Senate, July 25, with five dissenting votes.*

✓          ✓          ✓

* Richardson, ed., *Messages and Addresses of the Presidents*, Vol. VI, p. 430.

## THE CRITTENDEN RESOLUTIONS

*Resolved by the House of Representatives of the Congress of the United States,* That the present deplorable civil war has been forced upon the country by the disunionists of the Southern States now in revolt against the constitutional Government and in arms around the capital; that in this national emergency Congress, banishing all feelings of mere passion or resentment, will recollect only its duty to the whole country; that this war is not waged upon our part in any spirit of oppression, nor for any purpose of conquest or subjugation, nor purpose of overthrowing or interfering with the rights or established institutions of those States, but to defend and maintain the supremacy of the Constitution and to preserve the Union, with all the dignity, equality, and rights of the several States unimpaired; and that as soon as these objects are accomplished the war ought to cease.

## THE JOHNSON RESOLUTIONS

*Resolved,* That the present deplorable civil war has been forced upon the country by the disunionists of the Southern States now in revolt against the constitutional Government and in arms around the capital; that in this national emergency Congress, banishing all feeling of mere passion or resentment, will recollect only its duty to the whole country; that this war is not prosecuted upon our part in any spirit of oppression, nor for any purpose of conquest or subjugation, nor purpose of overthrowing or interfering with the rights or established institutions of those States, but to defend and maintain the supremacy of the Constitution and all laws made in pursuance thereof and to preserve the Union, with all the dignity, equality, and rights of the several States unimpaired; that as soon as these objects are accomplished the war ought to cease.

# — 16 —

# Lincoln: MESSAGE TO CONGRESS, July 4, 1861 *

*By proclamation of April 15, 1861, Lincoln called Congress to meet in special session July 4, 1861. In the intervening period Lincoln had strained the executive authority in his effort to suppress the rebellion. The Special Session Message informed Congress of the steps that the executive had taken and made specific recommendations for the grant of additional powers. It presented, in a more elaborate form than the Inaugural Address, Lincoln's conception of the significance of the struggle for the preservation of the Union in the light of world history.*

✦          ✦          ✦

FELLOW-CITIZENS OF THE SENATE AND HOUSE OF REPRESENTATIVES:—Having been convened on an extraordinary occasion, as authorized by the Constitution, your attention is not called to any ordinary subject of legislation.

At the beginning of the present Presidential term, four months ago, the functions of the Federal Government were found to be generally suspended within the several States of South Carolina, Georgia, Alabama, Mississippi, Louisiana, and Florida, excepting only those of the Post-office Department. . . .

. . . The purpose to sever the Federal Union was openly avowed. In accordance with this purpose, an ordinance had been adopted in each of these States, declaring the States respectively to be separated from the national Union. A formula for instituting a combined government of these States had been promulgated; and this illegal organization, in the character of confederate

* Richardson, ed., *Messages and Papers of the Confederacy,*
   Vol. VI, pp. 20 ff.

States, was already invoking recognition, aid, and intervention from foreign powers. . . .

And this issue embraces more than the fate of these United States. It presents to the whole family of man the question whether a constitutional republic or democracy —a government of the people by the same people—can or cannot maintain its territorial integrity against its own domestic foes. It presents the question whether discontented individuals, too few in number to control administration according to organic laws in any case, can always, upon the pretenses made in this case, or on any other pretenses, or arbitrarily without any pretense, break up their government, and thus practically put an end to free government upon the earth. It forces us to ask: Is there in all republics this inherent and fatal weakness? Must a government, of necessity, be too strong for the liberties of its own people, or too weak to maintain its own existence?

So viewing the issue, no choice was left but to call out the war power of the government, and so to resist force employed for its destruction by force for its preservation. . . .

It might seem, at first thought, to be of little difference whether the present movement at the South be called "secession" or "rebellion." The movers, however, well understand the difference. At the beginning they knew they could never raise their treason to any respectable magnitude by any name which implies violation of law. They knew their people possessed as much of moral sense, as much of devotion to law and order, and as much pride in and reverence for the history and government of their common country as any other civilized and patriotic people. They knew they could make no advancement directly in the teeth of these strong and noble sentiments. Accordingly, they commenced by an insidious debauching of the public mind. They invented an ingenious sophism which, if conceded, was followed by perfectly logical steps, through all the incidents, to the complete destruction of the Union. The sophism itself is that any State of the Union may consistently with the national Constitution, and therefore lawfully and peacefully, withdraw from the Union without the consent of the Union or of any other State. . . .

This sophism derives much, perhaps the whole, of its

currency from the assumption that there is some omnip-
otent and sacred supremacy pertaining to a State—to each
State of our Federal Union. Our States have neither more
nor less power than that reserved to them in the Union
by the Constitution—no one of them ever having been a
State out of the Union. The original ones passed into the
Union even before they cast off their British colonial
dependence; and the new ones each came into the Union
directly from a condition of dependence, excepting Texas.
And even Texas in its temporary independence was never
designated a State. The new ones only took the designa-
tion of States on coming into the Union, while that name
was first adopted for the old ones in and by the Declaration of Independence. . . . Having never been States
either in substance or in name outside of the Union,
whence this magical omnipotence of "State rights," assert-
ing a claim of power to lawfully destroy the Union itself?
Much is said about the "sovereignty" of the States; but
the word even is not in the national Constitution, nor, as
is believed, in any of the State constitutions. What is
"sovereignty" in the political sense of the term? Would it
be far wrong to define it as "a political community without a political superior"? Tested by this, no one of our
States except Texas ever was a sovereignty. . . . The
States have their status in the Union, and they have no
other legal status. If they break from this, they can only
do so against law and by revolution. The Union, and not
themselves separately, procured their independence and
their liberty. By conquest or purchase the Union gave
each of them whatever of independence or liberty it has.
The Union is older than any of the States, and, in fact,
it created them as States. Originally some dependent
colonies made the Union, and, in turn, the Union threw
off their old dependence for them, and made them States,
such as they are. Not one of them ever had a State constitution independent of the Union. Of course, it is not
forgotten that all the new States framed their constitutions
before they entered the Union—nevertheless, dependent
upon and preparatory to coming into the Union. . . .

What is now combated is the position that secession is
consistent with the Constitution—is lawful and peaceful.
It is not contended that there is any express law for it;
and nothing should ever be implied as law which leads to
unjust or absurd consequences. . . .

It may well be questioned whether there is to-day a majority of the legally qualified voters of any State except perhaps South Carolina in favor of disunion. There is much reason to believe that the Union men are the majority in many, if not in every other one, of the so-called seceded States. . . .

This is essentially a people's contest. On the side of the Union it is a struggle for maintaining in the world that form and substance of government whose leading object is to elevate the condition of men—to lift artificial weights from all shoulders; to clear the paths of laudable pursuit for all; to afford all an unfettered start, and a fair chance in the race of life. Yielding to partial and temporary departures, from necessity, this is the leading object of the government for whose existence we contend. . . .

Our popular government has often been called an experiment. Two points in it our people have already settled —the successful establishing and the successful administering of it. One still remains—its successful maintenance against a formidable internal attempt to overthrow it. It is now for them to demonstrate to the world that those who can fairly carry an election can also suppress a rebellion; that ballots are the rightful and peaceful successors of bullets; and that when ballots have fairly and constitutionally decided, there can be no successful appeal back to bullets; that there can be no successful appeal, except to ballots themselves, at succeeding elections. Such will be a great lesson of peace: teaching men that what they cannot take by an election, neither can they take it by war; teaching all the folly of being the beginners of a war. . . .

## Part III

# THE CONDUCT OF THE WAR

## — 17 —

## Lincoln: MESSAGES TO CONGRESS ON COMPENSATED EMANCIPATION, March 6 and December 1, 1862*

*"If I could save the Union without freeing any slaves,
I would do it. . . . My paramount object is to save the
Union." So wrote Lincoln to Greeley in August, 1862. But
even before that time, it had become clear that saving
the Union involved freeing the slaves. How this was to be
done, by whom it was to be done, when it was to be done
—all these remained to be worked out. From the beginning, Lincoln hoped that emancipation could be carried
through without violence or coercion and with the co-
operation of those slave states which had not seceded
from the Union. His first proposal was for compensated
emancipation and to this he returned again and again. In
his message of December, 1861, he recommended the
plan to the border states, but with no success. He returned
to it again in his message of March 6, 1862. Shortly after
that message, Lincoln summoned members of Congress
from the border states and appealed to them for support;
again he was disappointed. On July 12 of that year, he
held a conference with border state Congressmen and
read to them an appeal for cooperation, once again with-*

* Richardson, ed., *Messages and Papers,* Vol. VI, pp. 68 ff.,
126 ff.

*out result. The annual message of December 1 contained a specific plan for compensated emancipation and a moving appeal to nobly save rather than meanly lose "the last best hope of earth."*

✓ ✓ ✓

March 6, 1862

FELLOW-CITIZENS OF THE SENATE AND HOUSE OF REPRESENTATIVES:—I recommend the adoption of a joint resolution by your honorable bodies which shall be substantially as follows:

"*Resolved,* That the United States ought to co-operate with any State which may adopt gradual abolishment of slavery, giving to such State pecuniary aid, to be used by such State, in its discretion, to compensate for the inconveniences, public and private, produced by such change of system."

If the proposition contained in the resolution does not meet the approval of Congress and the country, there is the end; but if it does command such approval, I deem it of importance that the States and people immediately interested should be at once distinctly notified of the fact, so that they may begin to consider whether to accept or reject it. The Federal Government would find its highest interest in such a measure, as one of the most efficient means of self-preservation. The leaders of the existing insurrection entertain the hope that this government will ultimately be forced to acknowledge the independence of some part of the disaffected region, and that all the slave States north of such part will then say, "The Union for which we have struggled being already gone, we now choose to go with the Southern section." To deprive them of this hope substantially ends the rebellion, and the initiation of emancipation completely deprives them of it as to all the States initiating it. The point is not that *all* the States tolerating slavery would very soon, if at all, initiate emancipation; but that, while the offer is equally made to all, the more northern shall by such initiation make it certain to the more southern that in no event will the former ever join the latter in their proposed confederacy. I say "initiation" because, in my judgment, gradual and not sudden emancipation is better for all. In the mere financial or pecuniary view, any member of Congress with the census tables and treasury reports before him can readily see for himself how very soon the current expenditures of this war would purchase, at fair valuation, all the slaves in any named State. Such a proposition on the part of the General Government sets up no claim of a right by Federal authority to interfere with slavery within State limits, referring, as it does, the absolute control of the subject in each case to the State and its people immediately interested. It is proposed as a matter of perfectly free choice with them. . . .

The proposition now made (though an offer only), I hope it may be esteemed no offense to ask whether the pecuniary consideration tendered would not be of more value to the States and private persons concerned than are the institution and property in it in the present aspect of affairs.

While it is true that the adoption of the proposed resolution would be merely initiatory, and not within itself a practical measure, it is recommended in the hope that it would soon lead to important practical results. In full view of my great responsibility to my God and to my country, I earnestly beg the attention of Congress and the people to the subject.

ABRAHAM LINCOLN.

December 1, 1862

. . . Our strife pertains to ourselves—to the passing generations of men—and it can without convulsion be hushed forever with the passing of one generation.

In this view I recommend the adoption of the following resolution and articles amendatory to the Constitution of the United States:

*Resolved by the Senate and House of Representatives of the United States of America, in Congress assembled, (two-thirds of both Houses concurring)*, That the following articles be proposed to the Legislatures (or conventions) of the several States as amendments to the Constitution of the United States, all or any of which articles, when ratified by three fourths of the said Legislatures (or conventions), to be valid as part or parts of the said Constitution, viz:

ART.—. Every State wherein slavery now exists which shall abolish the same therein at any time or times before the 1st day of January, A.D. 1900, shall receive compensation from the United States as follows, . . .

ART.——. All slaves who shall have enjoyed actual freedom by the chances of the war at any time before the end of the rebellion shall be forever free; but all owners of such who shall not have been disloyal shall be compensated for them at the same rates as is provided for States adopting abolishment of slavery, but in such way that no slave shall be twice accounted for.

ART.——. Congress may appropriate money and otherwise provide for colonizing free colored persons with their own consent at any place or places without the United States.

I beg indulgence to discuss these proposed articles at some length. Without slavery the rebellion could never have existed; without slavery it could not continue.

Among the friends of the Union there is great diversity of sentiment and of policy in regard to slavery and the African race amongst us. Some would perpetuate slavery; some would abolish it suddenly and without compensation; some would abolish it gradually and with compensation; some would remove the freed people from us, and some would retain them with us; and there are yet other minor diversities. Because of these diversities we waste much strength in struggles among ourselves. By mutual concession we should harmonize and act together. This would be compromise, but it would be compromise among the friends and not with the enemies of the Union. These articles are intended to embody a plan of such mutual concessions. If the plan shall be adopted, it is assumed that emancipation will follow, at least in several of the States.

As to the first article, the main points are, first, the emancipation; secondly, the length of time for consummating it (thirty-seven years); and, thirdly, the compensation.

The emancipation will be unsatisfactory to the advocates of perpetual slavery, but the length of time should greatly mitigate their dissatisfaction. The time spares both races from the evils of sudden derangement—in fact, from the necessity of any derangement—while most of those whose habitual course of thought will be disturbed by the measure will have passed away before its consummation. They will never see it. Another class will hail the prospect of emancipation, but will deprecate the length of time. They will feel that it gives too little to the now living slaves. But it really gives them much. It saves them from the vagrant destitution which must largely attend immediate emancipation in localities where their numbers are very great, and it gives the inspiring assurance that their posterity shall be free forever. The plan leaves to each State choosing to act under it to abolish slavery now or at the end of the century, or at any intermediate time, or by degrees extending over the whole or any part of the period, and it obliges no two States to proceed alike. It also provides for compensation, and generally the mode of making it. This, it would seem, must further mitigate the dissatisfaction of those who favor perpetual slavery, and especially of those who are to receive the compensation. . . .

And if with less money, or money more easily paid, we can preserve the benefits of the Union by this means than we can by the war alone, is it not also economical to do it? Let us consider it, then. Let us ascertain the sum we have expended in the war since compensated emancipation was proposed last March, and consider whether if that measure had been promptly accepted by even some of the slave States the same sum would not have done more to close the war than has been otherwise done. If so, the measure would save money, and in that view would be a prudent and economical measure. . . . The aggregate sum necessary for compensated emancipation of course would be large. But it would require no ready cash, nor the bonds even any faster than the emancipation progresses. This might not, and porbably would not, close before the end of the thirty-seven years. At that time we shall probably have a hundred millions of people to share the burden, instead of thirty-one millions as now. . . .

The proposed emancipation would shorten the war, perpetuate peace, insure this increase of population, and proportionately the wealth of the country. With these we should pay all the emancipation would cost, together with our other debt, easier than we should pay our other debt without it. . . .

The third article relates to the future of the freed people. It does not oblige, but merely authorizes Congress to aid in colonizing such as may consent. This ought not to be regarded as objectionable on the one hand or on the other, insomuch as it comes to nothing unless by the mutual consent of the people to be deported and the

American voters through their representatives in Congress. . . .

The plan consisting of these articles is recommended, not but that a restoration of the national authority would be accepted without its adoption.

Nor will the war nor proceedings under the proclamation of September 22, 1862, be stayed because of the *recommendation* of this plan. Its timely *adoption,* I doubt not, would bring restoration, and thereby stay both.

And notwithstanding this plan, the recommendation that Congress provide by law for compensating any State which may adopt emancipation before this plan shall have been acted upon is hereby earnestly renewed. Such would be only an advance part of the plan, and the same arguments apply to both.

This plan is recommended as a means, not in exclusion of, but additional to, all others for restoring and preserving the national authority throughout the Union. The subject is presented exclusively in its economical aspect. The plan would, I am confident, secure peace more speedily and maintain it more permanently than can be done by force alone, while all it would cost, considering amounts and manner of payment and times of payment, would be easier paid than will be the additional cost of the war if we rely solely upon force. It is much, very much, that it would cost no blood at all.

The plan is proposed as permanent constitutional law. It cannot become such without the concurrence of, first, two thirds of Congress, and afterwards three fourths of the States. The requisite three fourths of the States will necessarily include seven of the slave States. Their concurrence, if obtained, will give assurance of their severally adopting emancipation at no very distant day upon the new constitutional terms. This assurance would end the struggle now and save the Union forever. . . .

Fellow-citizens, *we* can not escape history. We of this Congress and this administration will be remembered in spite of ourselves. No personal significance or insignificance can spare one or another of us. The fiery trial through which we pass will light us down in honor or dishonor to the latest generation. We *say* we are for the Union. The world will not forget that we say this. We know how to save the Union. The world knows we do know how to save it. We, even *we here,* hold the power and bear the responsibility. In *giving* freedom to the *slave* we *assure* freedom to the *free*—honorable alike in what we give and what we preserve. We shall nobly save or meanly lose the last, best hope of earth. Other means may succeed; this could not fail. The way is plain, peaceful, generous, just—a way which if followed the world will forever applaud and God must forever bless.

ABRAHAM LINCOLN.

# — 18 —

## UNION OR EMANCIPATION *

*Northern opinion was substantially united on the objective of the preservation of the Union, but it was at that time as much divided on the solution of the Negro problem as American opinion is today. At one extreme were those who thought that the nation had no power to interfere with slavery anywhere in the states, and who had no desire to see such power granted to the nation. At the other extreme were those who wished no union with slave owners on any terms, and who would rather see the Union severed than re-established with slavery existing anywhere on its soil. In between these extremes were all shades of opinion, moderate and immoderate. It was Lincoln's task if not to reconcile all these views at least to persuade those who held them to unite on the great objective of winning the War.*

*Horace Greeley, powerful editor of the New York Tribune, was a spokesman for one of these extreme groups. As early as 1860 he had advised letting "the erring sisters go in peace." Now he demanded—on behalf of 20 millions—that Lincoln transform the War into an abolitionist crusade. Lincoln's reply to this presumptuous letter is one of his most notable wartime pronouncements.*

✓              ✓              ✓

* Frank Moore, ed., *The Rebellion Record* (New York, 1871), Vol. XII, pp. 480 ff.

## A. "The Prayer of Twenty Millions"

August 19, 1862

DEAR SIR: . . . We complain that the Union cause has suffered, and is now suffering immensely, from mistaken deference to rebel Slavery. Had you, sir, in your Inaugural Address, unmistakably given notice that, in case the rebellion already commenced, were persisted in, and your efforts to preserve the Union and enforce the laws should be resisted by armed force, *you would recognize no loyal person as rightfully held in Slavery by a traitor,* we believe the rebellion would therein have received a staggering if not fatal blow. . . .

On the face of this wide earth, Mr. President, there is not one disinterested, determined, intelligent champion of the Union cause who does not feel that all attempts to put down the rebellion and at the same time uphold its inciting cause are preposterous and futile—that the rebellion, if crushed out to-morrow, would be renewed within a year if Slavery were left in full vigor—that army officers who remain to this day devoted to Slavery can at best be but half-way loyal to the Union—and that every hour of deference to Slavery is an hour of added and deepened peril to the Union. I appeal to the testimony of your ambassadors in Europe. It is freely at your service, not at mine. Ask them to tell you candidly whether the seeming subserviency of your policy to the slaveholding, slavery-upholding interest, is not the perplexity, the despair of statesmen of all parties, and be admonished by the general answer!

I close as I began with the statement that what an immense majority of the loyal millions of your countrymen require of you is a frank, declared, unqualified, ungrudging execution of the laws of the land, more especially of the Confiscation Act. That act gives freedom to the slaves of rebels coming within our lines, or whom those lines may at any time inclose—we ask you to render it due obedience by publicly requiring all your subordinates to recognize and obey it. The rebels are everywhere using the late anti-Negro riots in the North, as they have long used your officers' treatment of Negroes in the South, to convince the slaves that they have nothing to hope from a Union success—that we mean in that case to sell them into a bitter bondage to defray the cost of the war. Let them impress this as a truth on the great mass of their ignorant and credulous bondmen, and the Union will never be restored—never. We cannot conquer ten millions of people united in solid phalanx against us, powerfully aided by Northern sympathizers and European allies. We must have scouts, guides, spies, cooks, teamsters, diggers, and choppers from the blacks of the South, whether we allow them to fight for us or not, or we shall be baffled and repelled. As one of the millions who would gladly have avoided this struggle at any sacrifice but that of principle and honor, but who now feel that the triumph of the Union is indispensable not only to the existence of our country but to the well-being of mankind, I entreat you to render a hearty and unequivocal obedience to the law of the land.

Yours,
HORACE GREELEY

## B. "I Would Save the Union"

EXECUTIVE MANSION, WASHINGTON, August 22, 1862
*Hon. Horace Greeley:*

DEAR SIR: I have just read yours of the nineteenth, addressed to myself through the New-York *Tribune.* If there be in it any statements or assumptions of fact which I may know to be erroneous, I do not now and here controvert them. If there be in it any inferences which I may believe to be falsely drawn, I do not now and here argue against them. If there be perceptible in it an impatient and dictatorial tone, I waive it in deference to an old friend, whose heart I have always supposed to be right.

As to the policy I "seem to be pursuing," as you say, I have not meant to leave any one in doubt.

I would save the Union. I would save it the shortest way under the Constitution. The sooner the National authority can be restored, the nearer the Union will be "the Union as it was." If there be those who would not save the Union unless they could at the same time *save* Slavery, I do not agree with them. If there be those who would not save the Union unless they could at the same time *destroy* Slavery, I do not agree with them. My paramount object in this struggle *is* to save the Union, and is *not* either to save or destroy Slavery. If I could save the Union without freeing *any* slave, I would do it; and if I could save it by freeing *all* the slaves, I would do it; and if I could do it by freeing some and leaving others alone, I would also do that. What I do about Slavery and the colored race, I do because I believe it helps to save this Union; and what I forbear, I forbear because I do *not* believe it would help to save the Union. I shall do *less* whenever I shall believe what I am doing hurts the cause, and I shall do *more* whenever I shall believe doing more will help the cause. I shall try to correct errors when shown to be errors; and I shall adopt new views so fast as they shall appear to be true views. I have here stated my purpose according to my view of *official* duty, and I intend no modification of my oft-expressed *personal* wish that all men, everywhere, could be free.

Yours,
A. LINCOLN

## — 19 —

# EMANCIPATION

## A. The Emancipation Proclamation, January 1, 1863 *

*As early as July 22, 1862, Lincoln had read to his Cabinet a preliminary draft of an emancipation proclamation. At this time Secretary Seward suggested that the proclamation should not be issued until a military victory had been won. The battle of Antietam gave Lincoln his desired opportunity; on September 22 he read to his Cabinet a second draft of the proclamation. After some modifications this was issued as a preliminary proclamation; the formal and definite proclamation came January 1, 1863. This proclamation was particularly important in its effect upon European, and especially English, public opinion.*

✔        ✔        ✔

* *U. S. Statutes at Large*, Vol. XII, pp. 1268-1269.

By the President of the United
States of America:
*A Proclamation.*

Whereas on the 22d day of September, A.D. 1862, a proclamation was issued by the President of the United States, containing among other things, the following, to wit:

"That on the 1st day of January, A.D. 1863, all persons held as slaves within any State or designated part of a State the people whereof shall then be in rebellion against the United States shall be then, thenceforward, and forever free; and the executive government of the United States, including the military and naval authority thereof, will recognize and maintain the freedom of such persons and will do no act or acts to repress such persons, or any of them, in any efforts they may make for their actual freedom.

"That the executive will on the 1st day of January, aforesaid, by proclamation, designate the States and parts of States, if any, in which the people thereof, respectively, shall then be in rebellion against the United States; and the fact that any State or the people thereof shall on that day be in good faith represented in the Congress of the United States by members chosen thereto at elections wherein a majority of the qualified voters of such States shall have participated shall, in the absence of strong countervailing testimony, be deemed conclusive evidence that such State and the people thereof are not then in rebellion against the United States."

Now, therefore, I, Abraham Lincoln, President of the United States, by virtue of the power in me vested as Commander-in-Chief of the Army and Navy of the United States in time of actual armed rebellion against the authority and government of the United States, and as a fit and necessary war measure for suppressing said rebellion, do, on this 1st day of January, A.D. 1863, and in accordance with my purpose so to do, publicly proclaimed for the full period of one hundred days from the first day above mentioned, order and designate as the States and parts of States wherein the people thereof, respectively, are this day in rebellion against the United States the following, to wit:

Arkansas, Texas, Louisiana (except the parishes of St.

Bernard, Plaquemines, Jefferson, St. John, St. Charles, St. James, Ascension, Assumption, Terrebonne, Lafourche, St. Mary, St. Martin, and Orleans, including the city of New Orleans), Mississippi, Alabama, Florida, Georgia, South Carolina, North Carolina, and Virginia (except the forty-eight counties designated as West Virginia, and also the counties of Berkeley, Accomac, Northhampton, Elizabeth City, York, Princess Anne, and Norfolk, including the cities of Norfolk and Portsmouth), and which excepted parts are for the present left precisely as if this proclamation were not issued.

And by virtue of the power and for the purpose aforesaid, I do order and declare that all persons held as slaves within said designated states and parts of States are, and henceforward shall be, free; and that the Executive Government of the United States, including the military and naval authorities thereof, will recognize and maintain the freedom of said persons.

And I hereby enjoin upon the people so declared to be free to abstain from all violence, unless in necessary self-defense; and I recommend to them that, in all cases when allowed, they labor faithfully for reasonable wages.

And I further declare and make known that such persons of suitable condition will be received into the armed service of the United States to garrison forts, positions, stations, and other places, and to man vessels of all sorts in said service.

And upon this act, sincerely believed to be an act of justice, warranted by the Constitution upon military necessity, I invoke the considerate judgment of mankind and the gracious favor of Almighty God.

## B. The Thirteenth Amendment, December 18, 1865*

*There was from the beginning some question about the constitutionality of this proclamation. How far did presidential power extend even in time of war? Nor did the proclamation satisfy those who were determined to end slavery; after all, it did not affect the institution of slavery in those states which had not seceded from the Union. Clearly, something more was necessary than this limited wartime measure. The only satisfactory solution was to outlaw slavery by constitutional amendment. The Thir-*

* The Constitution of the United States.

*teenth Amendment, which did this, was proposed by Congress on February 1, 1865, ratified by 27 states, and went into effect December 18, 1865.*

✓          ✓          ✓

SEC. 1 Neither slavery nor involuntary servitude, except as a punishment for crime whereof the party shall have been duly convicted shall exist within the United States, or any place subject to their jurisdiction.

SEC. 2 Congress shall have power to enforce this article by appropriate legislation.

# — 20 —

# PRESIDENT LINCOLN AND THE WORKING-MEN OF MANCHESTER, ENGLAND

*During the Civil War the English government preserved a cautious and judicious neutrality. The opinion of the governing classes—and of their great organs like* The Times—*was sympathetic to the Confederacy. The Times, for example, characterized the Emancipation Proclamation as "a very sad document," and the* Edinburgh Magazine *called it "monstrous, reckless, and devilish." But the working men of Manchester, many of them victims of the Union blockade of Southern cotton, were stirred and exalted by the prospect of emancipation in America. Their message to Lincoln assuring him of their support now that the War was officially directed to the abolition of slavery is one of the moving documents in the history of Anglo-American relations and so too is Lincoln's felicitous reply.*

✓          ✓          ✓

## A. Address to President Lincoln by the Working-Men of Manchester, England, December 31, 1862*

To Abraham Lincoln, President of the United States: As citizens of Manchester, assembled at the Free-Trade Hall, we beg to express our fraternal sentiments toward you and your country. We rejoice in your greatness as outgrowth of England, whose blood and language you share, whose orderly and legal freedom you have applied to new circumstances, over a region immeasurably greater than our own. We honor your Free States, as a singularly happy abode for the working millions where industry is honored. One thing alone has, in the past, lessened our sympathy with your country and our confidence in it—we mean the ascendency of politicians who not merely maintained negro slavery, but desired to extend and root it more firmly. Since we have discerned, however, that the victory of the free North, in the war which has so sorely distressed us as well as afflicted you, will strike off the fetters of the slave, you have attracted our warm and earnest sympathy. We joyfully honor you, as the President, and the Congress with you, for many decisive steps toward practically exemplifying your belief in the words of your great founders: "All men are created free and equal." You have procured the liberation of the slaves in the district around Washington, and thereby made the centre of your Federation visibly free. You have enforced the laws against the slave-trade, and kept up your fleet against it, even while every ship was wanted for service in your terrible war. You have nobly decided to receive ambassadors from the negro republics of Hayti and Liberia, thus forever renouncing that unworthy prejudice which refuses the rights of humanity to men and women on account of their color. In order more effectually to stop the slave-trade, you have made with our Queen a treaty, which your Senate has ratified, for the right of mutual search. Your Congress has decreed freedom as the law forever in the vast unoccupied or half unsettled Territories which are directly subject to its legislative power. It has offered pecuniary aid to all States which will enact emancipation locally, and has forbidden your Generals to restore fugitive slaves who seek their

* Frank Moore, ed., *The Rebellion Record,* Vol. VI, p. 344.

protection. You have entreated the slave-masters to accept these moderate offers; and after long and patient
waiting, you, as Commander-in-Chief of the Army, have
appointed to-morrow, the first of January, 1863, as the
day of unconditional freedom for the slaves of the rebel
States. Heartily do we congratulate you and your country
on this humane and righteous course. We assume that
you cannot now stop short of a complete uprooting of
slavery. It would not become us to dictate any details, but
there are broad principles of humanity which must guide
you. If complete emancipation in some States be deferred,
though only to a predetermined day, still in the interval,
human beings should not be counted chattels. Women
must have the rights of chastity and maternity, men the
rights of husbands, masters the liberty of manumission.
Justice demands for the black, no less than for the white,
the protection of law—that his voice be heard in your
courts. Nor must any such abomination be tolerated as
slave-breeding States, and a slave market—if you are to
earn the high reward of all your sacrifices, in the approval of the universal brotherhood and of the Divine
Father. It is for your free country to decide whether any
thing but immediate and total emancipation can secure
the most indispensable rights of humanity against the
inveterate wickedness of local laws and local executives.
We implore you, for your own honor and welfare, not to
faint in your providential mission. While your enthusiasm
is aflame, and the tide of events runs high, let the work
be finished effectually. Leave no root of bitterness to
spring up and work fresh misery to your children. It is a
mighty task, indeed, to reörganize the industry not only
of four millions of the colored race, but of five millions
of whites. Nevertheless, the vast progress you have made
in the short space of twenty months fills us with hope that
every stain on your freedom will shortly be removed, and
that the erasure of that foul blot upon civilization and
Christianity—chattel slavery—during your Presidency will
cause the name of Abraham Lincoln to be honored and
revered by posterity. We are certain that such a glorious
consummation will cement Great Britain to the United
States in close and enduring regards. Our interests, more-
over, are identified with yours. We are truly one people,
though locally separate. And if you have any ill-wishers
here, be assured they are chiefly those who oppose liberty

at home, and that they will be powerless to stir up quarrels between us, from the very day in which your country becomes, undeniably and without exception, the home of the free. Accept our high admiration of your firmness in upholding the proclamation of freedom.

## B. Lincoln's Reply to the Working-Men of Manchester, England,* January 19, 1863

To the Working-Men of Manchester: I have the honor to acknowledge the receipt of the address and resolutions which you sent me on the eve of the new year. When I came, on the 4th of March, 1861, through a free and constitutional election to preside in the Government of the United States, the country was found at the verge of civil war. Whatever might have been the cause, or whosoever the fault, one duty, paramount to all others, was before me, namely, to maintain and preserve at once the Constitution and the integrity of the Federal Republic. A conscientious purpose to perform this duty is the key to all the measures of administration which have been and to all which will hereafter be pursued. Under our frame of government and my official oath, I could not depart from this purpose if I would. It is not always in the power of governments to enlarge or restrict the scope of moral results which follow the policies that they may deem it necessary for the public safety from time to time to adopt.

I have understood well that the duty of self-preservation rests solely with the American people; but I have at the same time been aware that favor or disfavor of foreign nations might have a material influence in enlarging or prolonging the struggle with disloyal men in which the country is engaged. A fair examination of history has served to authorize a belief that the past actions and influences of the United States were generally regarded as having been beneficial toward mankind. I have, therefore, reckoned upon the forbearance of nations. Circumstances—to some of which you kindly allude—induce me especially to expect that if justice and good faith should be practised by the United States, they would encounter no hostile influence on the part of Great Britain. It is now a pleasant duty to acknowledge the demonstration you have given of your desire that a spirit of amity and peace

* *The Writings of Abraham Lincoln,* Constitutional ed., Vol. VI, p. 248.

toward this country may prevail in the councils of your Queen, who is respected and esteemed in your own country only more than she is by the kindred nation which has its home on this side of the Atlantic.

I know and deeply deplore the sufferings which the working-men at Manchester, and in all Europe, are called to endure in this crisis. It has been often and studiously represented that the attempt to overthrow this government, which was built upon the foundation of human rights, and to substitute for it one which should rest exclusively on the basis of human slavery, was likely to obtain the favor of Europe. Through the action of our disloyal citizens, the working-men of Europe have been subjected to severe trials, for the purpose of forcing their sanction to that attempt. Under the circumstances, I cannot but regard your decisive utterances upon the question as an instance of sublime Christian heroism which has not been surpassed in any age or in any country. It is indeed an energetic and reinspiring assurance of the inherent power of truth and of the ultimate and universal triumph of justice, humanity, and freedom. I do not doubt that the sentiments you have expressed will be sustained by your great nation; and, on the other hand, I have no hesitation in assuring you that they will excite admiration, esteem, and the most reciprocal feelings of friendship among the American people. I hail this interchange of sentiment, therefore, as an augury that whatever else may happen, whatever misfortune may befall your country or my own, the peace and friendship which now exist between the two nations will be, as it shall be my desire to make them, perpetual.

ABRAHAM LINCOLN.

# — 21 —

# Jefferson Davis: REPLY TO THE EMANCIPATION PROCLAMATION, January 12, 1863*

*To President Davis the Emancipation Proclamation was "the most execrable measure recorded in the history of guilty man"; it was, at the same time, "the fullest vindication of the wisdom of secession." In his message to the Confederate Congress some two weeks after the Proclamation, Davis congratulated the Southern people on what seemed to him a clear manifestation of desperation in the North.*

✓          ✓          ✓

. . . The public journals of the North have been received, containing a proclamation, dated on the 1st day of the present month, signed by the President of the United States, in which he orders and declares all slaves within ten of the States of the Confederacy to be free, except such as are found within certain districts now occupied in part by the armed forces of the enemy. We may well leave it to the instincts of that common humanity which a beneficent Creator has implanted in the breasts of our fellowmen of all countries to pass judgment on a measure by which several millions of human beings of an inferior race, peaceful and contented laborers in their sphere, are doomed to extermination, while at the same time they are encouraged to a general assassination of their masters by the insidious recommendation "to abstain from violence unless in necessary self-defense." Our

* *Jefferson Davis, Constitutionalist,* Dunbar Rowland, ed., Vol. V, pp. 409-411, 414-415. (Jackson: Mississippi Department of Archives and History, 1923.)

own detestation of those who have attempted the most execrable measure recorded in the history of guilty man is tempered by profound contempt for the impotent rage which it discloses. So far as regards the action of this Government on such criminals as may attempt its execution, I confine myself to informing you that I shall, unless in your wisdom you deem some other course more expedient, deliver to the several State authorities all commissioned officers of the United States that may hereafter be captured by our forces in any of the States embraced in the proclamation, that they may be dealt with in accordance with the laws of those States providing for the punishment of criminals engaged in exciting servile insurrection. The enlisted soldiers I shall continue to treat as unwilling instruments in the commission of these crimes, and shall direct their discharge and return to their homes on the proper and usual parole.

In its political aspect this measure possesses great significance, and to it in this light I invite your attention. It affords to our whole people the complete and crowning proof of the true nature of the designs of the party which elevated to power the present occupant of the Presidential chair at Washington and which sought to conceal its purpose by every variety of artful device and by the perfidious use of the most solemn and repeated pledges on every possible occasion. . . .

The people of this Confederacy, then, cannot fail to receive this proclamation as the fullest vindication of their own sagacity in foreseeing the uses to which the dominant party in the United States intended from the beginning to apply their power, nor can they cease to remember with devout thankfulness that it is to their own vigilance in resisting the first stealthy progress of approaching despotism that they owe their escape from consequences now apparent to the most skeptical. This proclamation will have another salutary effect in calming the fears of those who have constantly evinced the apprehension that this war might end by some reconstruction of the old Union or some renewal of close political relations with the United States. These fears have never been shared by me, nor have I ever been able to perceive on what basis they could rest. But the proclamation affords the fullest guarantee of the impossibility of such a result; it has established a state of things which can lead to but one of three possible consequences—the extermination of the slaves, the exile of the whole white population from the Confederacy, or absolute and total separation of these States from the United States. . . .

# — 22 —

# CAPTAIN WILKES SEIZES MASON AND SLIDELL, 1861*

*James Mason and John Slidell were Confederate commissioners to, respectively, Britain and France. Learning that they had left Havana for England, Captain Wilkes of the* San Jacinto *stopped the* Trent *and removed them, without specific instructions from his own government. His act was technically a violation of international law. He should have brought the* Trent *to an American port where a prize court would have adjudicated the case. What he did, however, was what the British themselves had done scores of times in the early years of the century. At first the British government did not hold Wilkes's act contrary to international law. But within a few days a wave of anger swept over England, and the government itself was moved by threats. The British government demanded that the United States release the prisoners and apologize for Captain Wilkes's action, and insisted on an immediate answer. Fortunately, the Prince Consort toned down Lord Russell's first letter; however, it still bore the appearance of an ultimatum. In the meantime, orders were issued to hold the fleet in readiness for action, thousands of soldiers were shipped over to Canada, and the export of war munitions to America was stopped for a time.*

*Lincoln and Seward were in a dilemma. If they did not satisfy Britain, they might find themselves with another*

* D. Macneil Fairfax, "Captain Wilkes's Seizure of Mason and Slidell," in *Battles and Leaders of the Civil War* (New York, 1884-1888), Vol. II, pp. 135-141.

*war on their hands. If they did, public opinion—which had made a hero of Wilkes—would be outraged. With guidance from Lincoln, Seward found a solution. He did not apologize, but congratulated England on at last adopting the principles of international law for which the United States had long contended; then he had Mason and Slidell shipped off to England. On the whole American public opinion was pleased; the English were satisfied. In the long run the* Trent *affair cleared the air; but Britain paid a high price for her insistence on a fine point of law in the lasting sense of resentment which was planted in America.*

✔        ✔        ✔

In October, 1861, the United States screw-sloop *San Jacinto,* of which Captain Charles Wilkes was commander and the writer was executive officer, on her return from the west coast of Africa, touched at the island of St. Thomas to coal ship. Here for the first time we learned of the presence in those waters of the Confederate cruiser *Sumter* (Captain Raphael Semmes). Captain Wilkes immediately determined to search for the enemy. At Cienfuegos, on the south coast of Cuba, he learned from the United States consul-general at Havana that Messrs. Mason and Slidell, Confederate commissioners to Europe, and their secretaries and families had recently reached that port from Charleston en route to England. He immediately put to sea, October 26th, with the purpose of intercepting the blockade runner which had brought them out. The commissioners . . . had run the Union blockade successfully . . . and had arrived . . . at Havana on the 17th. There we ascertained that their plan was to leave on the 7th of November in the English steamer *Trent* for St. Thomas on their way to England, and readily calculated when and where in the Bahama Channel we might intercept them. Meanwhile . . . Captain Wilkes continued his cruise after the *Sumter* along the north coast of Cuba, also running over to Key West in the hope of finding the *Powhatan* or some other steamer to accompany him to the Bahama Channel. . . . Here, 240 miles from Havana, and 90 miles from Sagua la Grande, where the channel contracts to the width of 15 miles, at noon on the 8th of November the *Trent* was sighted. . . .

It was evident, even at that early day, that the South had the sympathy of nearly all Europe—particularly of England and France. When Captain Wilkes first took me into his confidence, and told me what he purposed to do, I earnestly reminded him of the great risk of a war with these two Governments, supported as they were by powerful navies; and when we reached Key West I suggested that he consult with Judge Marvin, one of the ablest maritime lawyers. I soon saw, however, that he had made up his mind to intercept and capture the *Trent* as well as to take possession of the commissioners, and I therefore ceased to discuss the affair. . . .

As the *Trent* approached she hoisted English colors; whereupon our ensign was hoisted and a shot was fired across her bow. As she maintained her speed and showed no disposition to heave to, a shell was fired across her bow which brought her to. Captain Wilkes hailed that he intended to send a boat on board, and I then left with the second cutter.

The manner of heaving the *Trent* to evidently was galling to Captain Moir. When he did stop his steamer, he showed how provoked he was by impatiently singing out through his trumpet, "What do you mean by heaving my vessel to in this manner?" I felt that I must in every way conciliate him when I should get on board. Two boats had been equipped ready to lower and the officers and crews detailed to jump into them. These were not employed until later. The boat I took was a third one, and as the sea was smooth, but a few minutes elapsed before we reached the *Trent*. I instructed the boat's crew to remain alongside for orders, and, boarding the vessel, I was escorted by one of her officers to the upper or promenade deck and was introduced to Captain Moir. . . . I immediately asked if I might see his passenger-list, saying that I had information that Messrs. Mason and Slidell were on board. The mention of Mr. Slidell's name caused that gentleman to come up and say, "I am Mr. Slidell; do you want to see me?" Mr. Mason, whom I knew very well, also came up at the same time, thus relieving me from Captain Moir's refusal, which was very polite but very positive, that I could not under such circumstances be shown any list of passengers. . . . In the briefest time . . . I informed Captain Moir that I had been sent by my commander to arrest Mr. Mason and Mr. Slidell and their secretaries, and send them prisoners on board the United States war vessel near by.

As may readily be understood, when it was known why I had boarded the *Trent,* there was an outburst of rage and indignation from the passengers, who numbered nearly one hundred, many of them Southerners. The captain and the four gentlemen bore themselves with great composure, but the irresponsible lookers-on sang out, "Throw the d—— fellow overboard!" I called on Captain Moir to preserve order, but, for the benefit of the excited passengers, I reminded them that our every move was closely observed from the *San Jacinto* by spy-glasses (she was within hailing distance), that a heavy battery was bearing upon them, and that any indignity to any of her officers or crew then on board might lead to dreadful consequences. This, together with Captain Moir's excellent commanding manner, had a quieting effect. . . .

After order had been restored, we discussed the affair more generally, Captain Moir, however, scarcely joining in the conversation—always dignified and punctilious. . . . I carefully avoided giving offense, and confined myself strictly to the duty which had taken me on board. I was anxious that Mr. Slidell and Mr. Mason should not leave any of their luggage behind. Mrs. Slidell having asked me who commanded the *San Jacinto,* I replied, "Your old acquaintance, Captain Wilkes"; whereupon she expressed surprise that he should do the very thing the Confederates were hoping for—something to arouse England; . . . "Really," she added, "Captain Wilkes is playing into our hands!" . . .

After the first uproar had subsided, I sent the boat to Captain Wilkes to say that these gentlemen were all on board, and had objected to being sent to the *San Jacinto,* and that I must use force to accomplish my orders; I asked for a boat to carry them comfortably on board, another for their baggage, and a third to carry stores, which the paymaster's clerk, at Captain Wilkes's order, had already purchased from the steward of the *Trent,* to add to the comfort of the new guests.

When all was ready and the boats were in waiting, I notified both Mr. Mason and Mr. Slidell that the time had come to send them to the *San Jacinto.* They came quietly down to the main-deck, and there repeated that they would not go unless force was used—whereupon two officers, previously instructed, escorted each commissioner to the side, and assisted them into the comfortable cutter sent especially for them. . . .

When all was finished I went on board the *San Jacinto* and reported to Captain Wilkes that I had not taken the *Trent* as a prize, as he had instructed me to do, giving certain reasons, which satisfied him; for he replied, "inasmuch as you have not taken her, you will let her go" or "proceed on her voyage." . . . The reasons I assigned to Captain Wilkes for my action were: First, that the capture of the *Trent* would make it necessary to put a large prize crew (officers and men) on board, and thus materially weaken our battery for use at Port Royal; secondly, that as there were a large number of women and children and mails and specie bound to various ports, the capture would seriously inconvenience innocent persons and merchants; so that I had determined, before taking her, to lay these matters before him for more serious consideration.

I gave my real reasons some weeks afterward to Secretary Chase, whom I met by chance at the Treasury Department, he having asked me to explain why I had not literally obeyed Captain Wilkes's instructions. I told him that it was because I was impressed with England's sympathy for the South, and felt that she would be glad to have so good a ground to declare war against the United States. Mr. Chase seemed surprised, and exclaimed, "You have certainly relieved the Government from great embarrassment, to say the least."

I returned immediately to the *Trent* and informed Captain Moir that Captain Wilkes would not longer detain him, and he might proceed on his voyage. The steamers soon separated, and thus ended one of the most critical events of our civil war.

— 23 —

## James Russell Lowell: "SHALL IT BE LOVE, OR HATE, JOHN?"*

*Few American poets were better known or more respected in England than James Russell Lowell, who was later to be the American minister to the Court of Saint James's. "Jonathan to John," one of the most famous poems of the second series of* Biglow *Papers, was Lowell's reply to the British concerning their conduct in the* Trent *affair, but the* Biglow *Papers covered the whole ground of Anglo-American wartime relations. Widely read in America, it long retained popularity but, needless to say, never achieved a comparable popularity in Britain.*

✓        ✓        ✓

It don't seem hardly right, John,
   When both my hands was full,
To stump me to a fight, John,—
   Your cousin, tu, John Bull!
      Ole Uncle S. sez he, "I guess
      We know it now," sez he,
"The Lion's paw is all the law,
      Accordin' to J. B.,
      That's fit for you an' me!"

You wonder why we're hot, John?
   Your mark wuz on the guns,
The neutral guns, thet shot, John,
   Our brothers an' our sons:
      Ole Uncle S. sez he, "I guess
      There's human blood," sez he,

* James Russell Lowell, "Jonathan to John," *Poems.*

"By fits an' starts, in Yankee hearts,
　　Though 't may surprise J. B.
　More 'n it would you an' me." . . .

　　　　*　　　*　　　*

We own the ocean, tu, John:
　　You mus'n' take it hard,
Ef we can't think with you, John,
　　It's jest your own back yard.
　　　Ole Uncle S. sez he, "I guess
　　　Ef *thet's* his claim," sez he,
"The fencin'-stuff 'll cost enough
　　　To bust up friend J. B.,
　　　Ez wal ez you an' me!" . . .

　　　　*　　　*　　　*

We ain't so weak an' poor, John,
　　With twenty million people,
An' close to every door, John,
　　A school-house an' a steeple.
　　　Ole Uncle S. sez he, "I guess
　　　It is a fact," sez he,
"The surest plan to make a Man
　　　Is, think him so, J. B.,
　　　Ez much ez you or me!" . . .

We know we've got a cause, John,
　　Thet's honest, just, an' true;
We thought 't would win applause, John,
　　If nowheres else, from you.
　　　Ole Uncle S. sez he, "I guess
　　　His love of right," sez he,
"Hangs by a rotten fibre o' cotton:
　　　There's natur' in J. B.,
　　　Ez wal ez in you an' me!"

　　　　*　　　*　　　*

Shall it be love, or hate, John?
　　It's you thet's to decide;
Ain't *your* bonds held by Fate, John,
　　Like all the world's beside?
　　　Ole Uncle S. sez he, "I guess
　　　Wise men forgive," sez he,

> "But not forgit; an' some time yit
> Thet truth may strike J. B.,
> Ez wal ez you an' me!"

> God means to make this land, John,
> Clear thru, from sea to sea,
> Believe an' understand, John,
> The *wuth* o' bein' free.
> Ole Uncle S. sez he, "I guess
> God's price is high," sez he;
> "But nothin' else than wut he sells
> Wears long, an' thet J. B.
> May larn, like you an' me!"

# — 24 —

# LORD PALMERSTON AND LORD RUSSELL CONSIDER RECOGNITION OR MEDIATION, 1862*

*It was an article of faith with Southern leaders that "Cotton is King." It followed that European nations, particularly Britain and France, deprived of Southern cotton, would of necessity intervene to break the blockade and thus assure Southern victory. Even if Britain did not attempt anything this drastic, she would assuredly rally European opinion to force mediation upon the North— mediation which would almost certainly assure Southern independence. But these well-considered assumptions proved, in the end, to be mistaken. Normally, Britain did need cotton, but in 1861 she had abundant supplies*

* Spencer Walpole, *The Life of Lord John Russell* (London, 1889), Vol. II, pp. 349-350.

*on hand and imported more from Egypt; British official opinion did favor the South, but it also wished to avoid war or an interpretation of a blockade which might prove embarrassing to her at a later time. Yet for two years it was touch and go. Again and again Britain seemed on the verge of some kind of recognition or intervention— at the time of the* Trent *affair, again when Lee's victories in Virginia seemed to make clear that the South had "made a nation" and even as late as spring of 1863 when British aristocrats organized a Southern Independence Association and when English shipyards were building rams for the Southern navy.*

*This correspondence between Prime Minister Viscount Palmerston and Foreign Secretary Lord John Russell illuminates official British thinking on the question of intervention and mediation.*

✓          ✓          ✓

94 PICADILLY: September 14, 1862.

My dear Russell,—The detailed accounts given in the "Observer" today of the battles of August 29 and 30 between the Confederates and the Federals show that the latter got a very complete smashing; and it seems not altogether unlikely that still greater disasters await them, and that even Washington or Baltimore may fall into the hands of the Confederates.

If this should happen, would it not be time for us to consider whether in such a state of things England and France might not address the contending parties and recommend an arrangement upon the basis of separation? . . . —Yours sincerely,

PALMERSTON

GOTHA: September 17, 1862.

My dear Palmerston,—Whether the Federal army is destroyed or not, it is clear that it is driven back to Washington and has made no progress in subduing the insurgent states. Such being the case, I agree with you that the time is come for offering mediation to the United States government with a view to the recognition of the independence of the Confederates. I agree further, that, in case of failure, we ought ourselves to recognize the Southern states as an independent state. For the purpose of taking so important a step, I think we must have a meeting of the Cabinet. The 23rd or 30th would suit me for the meeting.

We ought then, if we agree on such a step, to propose it first to France, and then, on the part of England and France, to Russia and other powers as a measure decided upon by us.

We ought to make ourselves safe in Canada, not by sending more troops there, but by concentrating those we have in a few defensible posts before the winter sets in.

I hope to get home on Sunday, but a letter sent to the Foreign Office is sure to reach me.

[RUSSELL]

BROADLANDS: September 23, 1862.

My dear Russell,—Your plan of proceedings about the mediation between the Federals and Confederates seems to be excellent. Of course, the offer would be made to both the contending parties at the same time; for, though the offer would be as sure to be accepted by the Southerns as was the proposal of the Prince of Wales by the Danish Princess, yet, in the one case as in the other, there are certain forms which it is decent and proper to go through.

A question would occur whether, if the two parties were to accept the mediation, the fact of our mediating would not of itself be tantamount to an acknowledgment of the Confederates as an independent state.

Might it not be well to ask Russia to join England and France in the offer of mediation? . . .

We should be better without her in the mediation, because she would be too favorable to the North; but on the other hand her participation in the offer might render the North the more willing to accept it.

The after communication to the other European powers would be quite right, although they would be too many for mediation.

As to the time of making the offer, if France and Russia agree—and France, we know, is quite ready and only waiting for our concurrence—events may be taking place which might render it desirable that the offer should be made before the middle of October.

It is evident that a great conflict is taking place to the northwest of Washington, and its issue must have a great effect on the state of affairs. If the Federals sustain a great defeat, they may be at once ready for mediation, and the iron should be struck while it is hot. If, on the other hand, they should have the best of it, we may wait awhile and see what may follow. . . .

Yours sincerely,
PALMERSTON

October 2, 1862 *

My dear Russell,—I return you Granville's letter which contains much deserving of serious consideration. There is no doubt that the offer of mediation upon the basis of separation would be accepted by the South. Why should it not be accepted? It would give the South in principle the points for which they are fighting. The refusal, if refusal there was, would come from the North, who would be unwilling to give up the principle for which they have been fighting so long as they had a reasonable expectation that by going on fighting they could carry their point. The condition of things therefore which would be favourable to an offer of mediation would be great success of the South against the North. That state of things seemed ten days ago to be approaching. Its advance has been lately checked, but we do not yet know the real course of recent events, and still less can we foresee what is about to follow. Ten days or a fortnight more may throw a clearer light upon future prospects.

As regards possible resentment on the part of the Northerns following upon acknowledgment of the Independence of the South, it is quite true that we should have less to care about that resentment in the spring when communication with Canada was open, and when our naval force could more easily operate upon the American coast, than in winter when we are cut off from Canada and the American coast is not so safe.

But if the acknowledgment were made at one and the same time by England, France and some other Powers, the Yankees would probably not seek a quarrel with us alone, and would not like one against a European Confederation. Such a quarrel would render certain and permanent that Southern Independence the acknowledgment of which would have caused it.

The first communication to be made by England and France to the contending parties might be, not an absolute

* E. D. Adams, *Great Britain and the American Civil War* (New York, 1925), Vol. II, pp. 43-44.

offer of mediation but a friendly suggestion whether the time was not come when it might be well for the two parties to consider whether the war, however long continued, could lead to any other result than separation; and whether it might not therefore be best to avoid the great evils which must necessarily flow from a prolongation of hostilities by at once coming to an agreement to treat upon that principle of separation which must apparently be the inevitable result of the contest, however long it may last.

The best thing would be that the two parties should settle details by direct negotiation with each other, though perhaps with rancorous hatred now existing between them this might be difficult. But their quarrels in negotiation would do us no harm if they did not lead to a renewal of war. An armistice, if not accompanied by a cessation of blockades, would be all in favor of the North, especially if New Orleans remained in the hands of the North.

The whole matter is full of difficulty, and can only be cleared up by some more decided events between the contending armies. . . .

PALMERSTON


October 22, 1862 *

My dear Russell: . . . All that we could possibly do without injury to our position would be to ask the two Parties not whether they would agree to an armistice but whether they might not turn their thoughts towards an arrangement between themselves. But the answer of each might be written by us before hand. The Northerns would say that the only condition of arrangement would be the restoration of the Union; the South would say their only condition would be an acknowledgment by the North of Southern Independence.—We should not be more advanced and should only have pledged each party more strongly to the object for which they are fighting. I am therefore inclined to change the opinion on which I wrote to you when the Confederates seemed to be carrying all before them, and I am very much come back to our original view of the matter, that we must continue merely

* E. D. Adams, *Great Britain and the American Civil War* (New York, 1925), Vol. II, pp. 54-55.

to be lookers-on till the war shall have taken a more decided turn.

PALMERSTON

**Lord John Russell to Sir G. C. Lewis***

October 26, 1862

I am not lucky in making the present state of things in Europe understood. France is supposed to be friendly to recognition, Russia has made no sign of any kind; but neither with France nor Russia have I thought myself empowered to open any official correspondence until the Cabinet had sanctioned the purport of that correspondence. I have just read Gladstone's paper, and I agree in its main object. I am not disposed in any case to take up arms to settle the American war by force. But I think if the Great Powers of Europe were to offer their good offices, and those good offices were to be rejected by the North, we should be fairly entitled to chuse our own time to recognize the Southern states. The time most suitable for such an act would probably be at the commencement of the next campaign and when Parliament was sitting.

— 25 —

# Charles Francis Adams: "THIS IS WAR," September 5, 1863 †

*The last diplomatic crisis between Britain and the United States threatened to be the most serious. As early as 1861 the Confederate government had dispatched Captain Bulloch to England to contract for the construction of commerce-destroyers in British shipyards. English*

* G. P. Gooch, *The Later Correspondence of Lord John Russell* (London, 1925), Vol. II, pp. 328-329.
† Great Britain, Parliament. *Accounts and Papers. State Papers, North America* (1864) 62:17-18.

law, and the Proclamation of Neutrality, forbade this, but it was relatively easy to evade the prohibition by juggling the ownership papers.

Thus the Confederates were able to have the Florida and the Alabama built in England; the subsequent depredations of these ships laid the basis for the Alabama claims. That the Alabama was being built for the Confederacy was common knowledge, but when Minister Adams protested it, he was met with the assertion that there was no legal proof of Confederate ownership!

Equally serious was the Confederate plan to build iron-clad rams in British yards. Contracts for these were placed with the Laird brothers, for delivery in the summer of 1863, and construction was soon under way at Birkenhead. If these rams should get away, the prospects for American commerce were dark; there were no United States ships that could stand up to them. As Captain Gustavus Fox, Assistant Secretary of the Navy, wrote, "It is a question of life and death." Adams took energetic action, laying before Russell evidence of Confederate ownership, and a Congressional Act of March, 1863, which authorized Lincoln to issue letters of marque to merchantmen; the victims would obviously be English vessels.

On September 3, 1863, Russell ordered the ironclads to be detained. Adams did not know this, and two days later he sent this famous letter with its somewhat ambiguous threat of war. The letter was not essential, but it helped. In October the ironclads were seized by the British government and subsequently purchased by and commissioned into the British Navy.

LEGATION OF THE UNITED STATES, LONDON,
September 5, 1863

MY LORD: At this moment, when one of the iron-clad war-vessels is on the point of departure from this kingdom on its hostile errand against the United States, I am honoured with the reply of your Lordship to my notes of the 11th, 16th, and 25th of July and of the 14th of August. I trust I need not express how profound is my regret at the conclusion to which Her Majesty's Government have arrived. I can regard it no otherwise than as practically opening to the insurgents free liberty in this kingdom to execute a policy described in one of their late publications in the following language:—

"In the present state of the harbour-defences of New York, Boston, Portland, and smaller Northern cities, such a vessel as the 'Warrior' would have little difficulty in entering any of those ports, and inflicting a vital blow upon the enemy. The destruction of Boston alone would be worth a hundred victories in the field. It would bring such a terror to the 'blue-noses' as to cause them to wish eagerly for peace, despite their overweening love of gain which has been so freely administered to since the opening of this war. Vessels of the 'Warrior' class would promptly raise the blockade of our ports, and would, even in this respect, confer advantages which would soon repay the cost of their construction."

It would be superfluous in me to point out to your Lordship that this is war. No matter what may be the theory adopted of neutrality in a struggle, when this process is carried on in the manner indicated from a territory and with the aid of the subjects of a third party, that third party, to all intents and purposes, ceases to be neutral. Neither is it necessary to show that any Government which suffers it to be done fails in enforcing the essential conditions of international amity towards the country against whom the hostility is directed. In my belief it is impossible that any nation retaining a proper degree of self-respect could tamely submit to a continuance of relations so utterly deficient in reciprocity. I have no idea that Great Britain would do so for a moment.

After a careful examination of the full instructions with which I have been furnished in preparation for such an emergency, I deem it inexpedient for me to attempt any recurrence to arguments for effective interposition in the present case. The fatal objection of impotency which paralyzes Her Majesty's Government seems to present an insuperable barrier against all further reasoning. Under these circumstances I prefer to desist from communicating to your Lordship even such further portions of my existing instructions as are suited to the case, lest I should contribute to aggravate difficulties already far too serious. I therefore content myself with informing your Lordship that I transmit by the present steamer a copy of your note

for the consideration of my Government, and shall await
the more specific directions that will be contained in the
reply.

CHARLES FRANCIS ADAMS

— 26 —

# OUSTING THE FRENCH
# FROM MEXICO, 1862-1866

*The Civil War gave Napoleon III an opportunity to
do what Talleyrand and Canning had dreamed of: to
bring the New World into the balance of power and to
re-establish European authority in North America.*

*The decision of the Mexican Congress, in July, 1861,
to suspend all payments on foreign debts, brought to a
head a situation which had long been threatening. France,
Spain, and Great Britain signed an agreement for joint
intervention and in 1862 took possession of Mexican custom houses. Spain and Great Britain, reaching a satisfactory agreement with Mexico, then withdrew from the
coalition, leaving France in control of the situation. A
French army defeated Juarez, captured the Mexican capital, and organized a provisional government which
promptly voted to establish an Empire, and invited the
Austrian Archduke Maximilian to the throne. Secretary
Seward watched this violation of the Monroe Doctrine
with deep disapproval but hesitated to antagonize Emperor Napoleon III at this juncture. The dispatch of
March 3, 1862, sets forth the American position on intervention and assumes the honorable intentions of the sig-
natories of the convention of 1861. The success of the
Union arms by 1864 made Congress ready to take a
bolder position, but the resolution of April 4, 1864, was
not passed by the Senate. After the War, Seward assumed
a position of inflexible hostility to the maintenance of the
French regime in Mexico, and the dispatch of April 16,*

*1866, made clear that the United States would not toler-ate Austrian military support to Emperor Maximilian. French troops were finally withdrawn from Mexico in 1867 and in June of that year the hapless Maximilian was shot.*

✓                    ✓                    ✓

## A. Mr. Seward to Mr. Adams, March 3, 1862 *

DEPARTMENT OF STATE,
WASHINGTON, March 3, 1862.

Sir: We observe indications of a growing opinion in Europe that the demonstrations which are being made by Spanish, French, and British forces against Mexico are likely to be attended with a revolution in that country which will bring in a monarchical government there, in which the crown will be assumed by some foreign prince.

This country is deeply concerned in the peace of nations, and aims to be loyal at the same time in all its relations, as well to the allies as to Mexico. The President has therefore instructed me to submit his views on the new aspect of affairs to the parties concerned. He has relied upon the assurances given to this government by the allies that they were seeking no political objects and only a redress of grievances. He does not doubt the sincerity of the allies, and his confidence in their good faith, if it could be shaken, would be reinspired by explanations apparently made in their behalf that the governments of Spain, France, and Great Britain are not intending to intervene and will not intervene to effect a change of the constitutional form of government now existing in Mexico, or to produce any political change there in opposition to the will of the Mexican people. Indeed, he understands the allies to be unanimous in declaring that the proposed revolution in Mexico is moved only by Mexican citizens now in Europe.

The President, however, deems it his duty to express to the allies, in all candor and frankness, the opinion that no monarchical government which could be founded in Mexico, in the presence of foreign navies and armies in the waters and upon the soil of Mexico, would have any

* U. S. 37th Congress, 2d Session, *House Doc.* No. 100, pp. 207-208.

prospect of security or permanency. Secondly, that the instability of such a monarchy there would be enhanced if the throne should be assigned to any person not of Mexican nativity. That under such circumstances the new government must speedily fall unless it could draw into its support European alliances, which, relating back to the present invasion, would, in fact, make it the beginning of a permanent policy of armed European monarchical intervention injurious and practically hostile to the most general system of government on the continent of America, and this would be the beginning rather than the ending of revolution in Mexico.

These views are grounded upon some knowledge of the political sentiments and habits of society in America.

In such a case it is not to be doubted that the permanent interests and sympathies of this country would be with the other American republics. It is not intended on this occasion to predict the course of events which might happen as a consequence of the proceeding contemplated, either on this continent or in Europe. It is sufficient to say that, in the President's opinion, the emancipation of this continent from European control has been the principal feature in its history during the last century. It is not probable that a revolution in the contrary direction would be successful in an immediately succeeding century, while population in America is so rapidly increasing, resources so rapidly developing, and society so steadily forming itself upon principles of democratic American government. Nor is it necessary to suggest to the allies the improbability that European nations could steadily agree upon a policy favorable to such a counter-revolution as one conducive to their own interests, or to suggest that, however studiously the allies may act to avoid lending the aid of their land and naval forces to domestic revolutions in Mexico, the result would nevertheless be traceable to the presence of those forces there, although for a different purpose, since it may be deemed certain that but for their presence there no such revolution could probably have been attempted or even conceived.

The Senate of the United States has not, indeed, given its official sanction to the precise measures which the President has proposed for lending our aid to the existing government in Mexico, with the approval of the allies, to relieve it from its present embarrassments. This, however, is only a question of domestic administration. It would be very erroneous to regard such a disagreement as indicating any serious difference of opinion in this government or among the American people in their cordial good wishes for the safety, welfare, and stability of the republican system of government in that country.

I am, sir, your obedient servant,

WILLIAM H. SEWARD

## B. House Resolution on French Intervention in Mexico, April 4, 1864*

*Resolved.* That the Congress of the United States are unwilling, by silence, to leave the nations of the world under the impression that they are indifferent spectators of the deplorable events now transpiring in the Republic of Mexico; and they therefore think fit to declare that it does not accord with the policy of the United States to acknowledge a monarchical government, erected on the ruins of any republican government in America, under the auspices of any European power.

## C. Mr. Seward to Mr. Motley, April 16, 1866 †

DEPARTMENT OF STATE,

WASHINGTON, April 16, 1866.

Sir: I have had the honor to receive your despatch of the 27th of March, No. 155, which brings the important announcement that a treaty, called a "military supplementary convention," was ratified on the 15th of that month between the Emperor of Austria and the Prince Maximilian, who claims to be an emperor in Mexico.

You inform me that it is expected that about one thousand volunteers will be shipped (under this treaty) from Trieste to Vera Cruz very soon, and that at least as many more will be shipped in autumn.

I have heretofore given you the President's instructions to ask for explanations, and, conditionally, to inform the government of Austria that the despatch of military expeditions by Austria under such an arrangement as the one which seems now to have been consummated would be regarded with serious concern by the United States.

* E. McPherson, ed., *Political History of the Rebellion* (Washington, D. C., 1864), p. 349.

† U. S. 39th Congress, 1st Session, *House Doc.* No. 93, pp. 46-47.

The subject has now been further considered in connexion with the official information thus recently received. The time seems to have arrived when the attitude of this government in relation to Mexican affairs should be once again frankly and distinctly made known to the Emperor of Austria, and all other powers whom it may directly concern. The United States, for reasons which seem to them to be just, and to have their foundation in the laws of nations, maintain that the domestic republican government with which they are in relations of friendly communication is the only legitimate government existing in Mexico; that a war has for a period of several years been waged against that republic by the government of France; which war began with a disclaim of all political or dynastic designs that that war has subsequently taken upon itself, and now distinctly wears the character of an European intervention to overthrow that domestic republican government, and to erect in its stead a European, imperial, military despotism by military force. The United States, in view of the character of their own political institutions, their proximity and intimate relations towards Mexico, and their just influence in the political affairs of the American continent, cannot consent to the accomplishment of that purpose by the means described. The United States have therefore addressed themselves, as they think, seasonably to the government of France, and have asked that its military forces, engaged in that objectionable political invasion, may desist from further intervention and be withdrawn from Mexico.

A copy of the last communication upon this subject, which was addressed by us to the government of France, is herewith transmitted for your special information. This paper will give you the true situation of the question. It will also enable you to satisfy the government of Vienna that the United States must be no less opposed to military intervention for political objects hereafter in Mexico by the government of Austria, than they are opposed to any further intervention of the same character in that country by France.

You will, therefore, at as early a day as may be convenient, bring the whole case, in a becoming manner, to the attention of the imperial royal government. You are authorized to state that the United States sincerely desire that Austria may find it just and expedient to come upon the same ground of non-intervention in Mexico which is maintained by the United States, and to which they have invited France.

You will communicate to us the answer of the Austrian government to this proposition.

This government could not but regard as a matter of serious concern the despatch of any troops from Austria for Mexico while the subject which you are thus directed to present to the Austrian government remains under consideration.

I am, sir, your obedient servant,

WILLIAM H. SEWARD

# — 27 —

# Lincoln: THE GETTYSBURG ADDRESS, November 19, 1863*

*On July 4, Lincoln had announced to the country the victory of the Army of the Potomac and had invoked "the condolences of all for the many gallant fallen." That November, part of the battlefield of Gettysburg was made a permanent cemetery for the soldiers who had fallen there. Edward Everett of Massachusetts delivered the principal oration. The superintendent of the enterprise, David Wills, asked Lincoln to make "a few appropriate remarks," and the result was the most memorable of all American addresses.*

✦          ✦          ✦

Four score and seven years ago our fathers brought forth on this continent a new nation, conceived in Liberty, and dedicated to the proposition that all men are created equal.

Now we are engaged in a great civil war, testing

* Nicolay and Hay, eds., *The Complete Works of Abraham Lincoln* (New York, 1894), Vol. II, p. 439.

whether that nation or any nation so conceived and so dedicated can long endure. We are met on a great battle-field of that war. We have come to dedicate a portion of that field as a final resting place for those who here gave their lives that that nation might live. It is altogether fitting and proper that we should do this.

But in a larger sense we cannot dedicate—we cannot consecrate—we cannot hallow—this ground. The brave men, living and dead, who struggled here, have con-secrated it, far above our poor power to add or detract. The world will little note nor long remember what we say here, but it can never forget what they did here. It is for us the living, rather, to be dedicated here to the unfinished work which they who fought here have thus far so nobly advanced. It is rather for us to be here dedicated to the great task remaining before us—that from these honored dead we take increased devotion to that cause for which they gave the last full measure of devotion—that we here highly resolve that these dead shall not have died in vain—that this nation, under God, shall have a new birth of freedom—and that government of the people, by the people, for the people, shall not perish from the earth.

# Part IV

# INTERNAL PROBLEMS, NORTH AND SOUTH

## — 28 —

## KENTUCKY TRIES TO BE NEUTRAL, June 8, 1861 *

*The Border States—Maryland, Kentucky, Missouri, and eventually that part of Virginia which became West Virginia—represented a peculiar problem and a very special challenge to both Union and Confederacy. All of these were "slave" states; all of them except western Virginia were Southern in population and in sympathy. If these states went with the Confederacy, the task of the Union would be almost insuperable. Of all the Border States, Kentucky was clearly the most important. Conscious of her vulnerability, of her close economic ties with the North, and of her long tradition of nationalism, Kentucky was loathe to break her ties with the Union. Governor Beriah Magoffin, of Kentucky, though unquestionably Southern in sympathies, tried to maintain the neutrality of his state. He refused Lincoln's call for troops and the following week refused Davis's call for troops, but he permitted Southern recruiting agents to operate in the state. In mid-May both houses of the Kentucky legislature passed resolutions declaring the state's neutrality. Not content with this, Magoffin tried to persuade his neighboring states of Tennessee, Missouri, Indiana, and*

* Frank Moore, ed., *The Rebellion Record* (New York, 1861), Vol. I, pp. 353-356.

*Ohio to form a neutral block to mediate between North and South. Senator Crittenden's devotion to the Union was more sincere* (see Document No. 10). *Not only was he responsible for the Crittenden Compromise, but he was chairman of the convention of border slave states which met at Frankfort, Kentucky on May 27 "to consult on the critical condition of the country." This "Address to the People of Kentucky," pleading for neutrality, was drafted by him.*

✔          ✔          ✔

## TO THE PEOPLE OF KENTUCKY.

. . . Your State, on a deliberate consideration of her responsibilities—moral, political, and social—has determined that the proper course for her to pursue is to take no part in the controversy between the Government and the seceded States but that of *mediator* and *intercessor*. She is unwilling to take up arms against her brethren residing either North or South of the geographical line by which they are unhappily divided into warring sections. This course was commended to her by every consideration of patriotism, and by a proper regard for her own security. It does not result from timidity; on the contrary, it could only have been adopted by a brave people —so brave that the least imputation on their courage would be branded as false by their written and traditional history.

Kentucky was right in taking this position—because, from the commencement of this deplorable controversy, her voice was for reconciliation, compromise, and peace. She had no cause of complaint against the General Government, and made none. . . .

It is a proud and grand thing for Kentucky to stand up and say, as she can, truthfully, in the face of the world, "We had no hand in this thing; our skirts are clear." And, in looking at the *terrorism* that prevails elsewhere —beholding freedom of speech denied to American citizens, their homesteads subjected to lawless visitation, their property confiscated, and their persons liable to incarceration and search—how grandly does she not loom up, as she proclaims to the oppressed and miserable, We offer you a refuge! Here, constitutional law, and respect for individual rights, still exist! Here is an asylum where loyalty to the name, nation, and Flag of the Union predominates; and here is the only place, in this lately great Republic, where true freedom remains—that freedom for which our fathers fought—the citizen being free to speak, write, or publish any thing he may wish, responsible only to the laws, and not controlled by the violence of the mob.

Is not this an attitude worthy of a great people, and do not her position and safety require her to maintain it? If she deviates from it; if she suffers herself in a moment of excitement to be led off by sympathy with one side or the other—to ally herself with either section—inevitable and speedy ruin must fall upon her. What reason can be urged to incline her to such a fatal step? She is still, thank God, a member of the Union, owing constitutional allegiance to it—an allegiance voluntarily given, long maintained, and from which she has derived countless benefits. Can she, by her own act, forfeit this allegiance, and by the exercise of any constitutional power sever hefself from that Government? In our opinion the statement of the proposition insures its rejection. . . .

Under the National Government, she has a right to the protection of thirty-three great States, and with them, thus protected, can defy the world in arms. Under it, she becomes prosperous and happy. Deprived of it, she finds herself exposed to imminent danger. She has a border front on the Ohio River or near seven hundred miles, with three powerful States on that border. She has four hundred miles on the South by which she is separated from Tennessee by a merely conventional line. Her eastern front is on Virginia, and part of her western on Missouri —thus making her antagonistic, in the event of collision, to Virginia, which is our mother, and to Missouri, which is our daughter. Hemmed in thus on every side by powers —each one of which is equal to her own—her situation, and her sense of loyalty to the Union, imperatively demand of her to insist on the integrity of the Union, its Constitution, and Government. Peace is of vital consequence to her, and can only be secured to her by preserving the Union inviolate. Kentucky has no cause of quarrel with the Constitution, and no wish to quarrel with her neighbors; but abundant reason to love both. . . .

Kentucky, in so grave a matter as this, passes by mere legal technicalities and a discussion of theoretical difficulties of Government, poises herself upon her right to do what the necessities of her condition imperatively demanded of her, and relies upon the good sense and magnanimity of her sister States, seeing that there is no parallel in her condition and theirs to do her justice.

In all things she is as loyal as ever to the constitutional administration of the Government. She will follow the Stars and Stripes to the utmost regions of the earth, and defend them from foreign insult. She refuses allegiance with any who would destroy the Union. All she asks is permission to keep out of this unnatural strife. When called to take part in it, she believes there is more honor in the breach than in the observance of any supposed duty to perform it.

Feeling that she is clearly right in this, and has announced her intention to refrain from aggression upon others, she must protest against her soil being made the theatre of military operations by any belligerent. The war must not be transferred, by the warring sections, from their own to her borders. Such unfriendly action cannot be viewed with indifference by Kentucky. . . .

J. J. CRITTENDEN, Pres.
and others.

— 29 —

# WEST VIRGINIA BECOMES A STATE, 1861 *

*The problem of western Virginia was a peculiar one. Slavery had never firmly established itself in this mountainous country and although most of the inhabitants had come originally from Virginia, many of them had left the East in order to escape slavery. There was also a long record of discontent with the political and economic*

* Frank Moore, ed., *The Rebellion Record* (New York, 1861), Vol. I, pp. 403-404.

*dominance of the East. When Virginia seceded, the west-
ern counties refused to go along. It was a fateful act. A
Virginia state government, loyal to the Union, was organized at Wheeling and this government gave its consent—a
consent required by the Federal Constitution—to the crea-
tion of the State of West Virginia. That state was recognized and admitted to the Union on December 31, 1862.
We give here the "Declaration of the People of Va." at
the Wheeling Convention of June, 1861.*

✓          ✓          ✓

## DECLARATION OF THE PEOPLE OF VA.,

### REPRESENTED IN CONVENTION IN WHEELING, JUNE 17, 1861.

THE true purpose of all government is to promote the
welfare and provide for the protection and security of
the governed, and when any form of organization of government proves inadequate for, or subversive of this purpose, it is the right, it is the duty of the latter to alter or
abolish it. The Bill of Rights of Virginia, framed in 1776,
reaffirmed in 1830, and again in 1851, expressly reserves
this right to the majority of her people, and the existing
Constitution does not confer upon the General Assembly
the power to call a Convention to alter its provisions, or
to change the relations of the Commonwealth, without
the previously expressed consent of such a majority. The
act of the General Assembly, calling the Convention
which assembled at Richmond in February last, was
therefore a usurpation; and the Convention thus called
has not only abused the powers nominally intrusted to
it, but, with the connivance and active aid of the Executive, has usurped and exercised other powers, to the
manifest injury of the people, which, if permitted, will
inevitably subject them to a military despotism.

The Convention, by its pretended ordinances, has required the people of Virginia to separate from and wage
war against the Government of the United States, and
against the citizens of neighboring States, with whom they
have heretofore maintained friendly, social, and business
relations:

It has attempted to subvert the Union founded by
Washington and his co-patriots in the purer days of the
Republic, which has conferred unexampled prosperity

upon every class of citizens and upon every section of the country:

It has attempted to transfer the allegiance of the people to an illegal confederacy of rebellious States, and required their submission to its pretended edicts and decrees:

It has attempted to place the whole military force and military operations of the Commonwealth under the control and direction of such Confederacy, for offensive as well as defensive purposes:

It has, in conjunction with the State Executive, instituted wherever their usurped power extends, a reign of terror, intended to suppress the free expression of the will of the people, making elections a mockery and a fraud:

The same combination, even before the passage of the pretended Ordinance of Secession, instituted war by the seizure and appropriation of the property of the Federal Government, and by organizing and mobilizing armies, with the avowed purpose of capturing or destroying the Capital of the Union:

They have attempted to bring the allegiance of the people of the United States into direct conflict with their subordinate allegiance to the State, thereby making obedience to their pretended Ordinance treason against the former.

We, therefore, the delegates here assembled in Convention to devise such measures and take such action as the safety and welfare of the loyal citizens of Virginia may demand, having mutually considered the premises, and viewing with great concern the deplorable condition to which this once happy Commonwealth must be reduced, unless some regular adequate remedy is speedily adopted, and appealing to the Supreme Ruler of the Universe for the rectitude of our intentions, do hereby in the name and on the behalf of the good people of Virginia, solemnly declare, that the preservation of their dearest rights and liberties, and their security in person and property, imperatively demand the reorganization of the Government of the Commonwealth, and that all acts of said Convention and Executive, tending to separate this Commonwealth from the United States, or to levy and carry on war against them, are without authority and void; and the offices of all who adhere to the said Convention and Executive, whether legislative, executive, or judicial, are vacated.

## — 30 —

# EX PARTE MERRYMAN, 1861 *

*Nowhere in the Border States were Southern sympathizers more active than in Maryland; one of the most active was John Merryman, a citizen of Baltimore. In May, 1861, Merryman was arrested and imprisoned in Fort McHenry by military order. He promptly applied for writ of habeas corpus and, no ground having been shown for his arrest, Chief Justice Taney authorized the writ and commanded General Cadwalader to deliver up the prisoner. The General refused to respect the writ. The Chief Justice cited him for contempt of court, and the General refused to receive the writ of contempt. In these circumstances the Chief Justice filed his historic opinion in the case of Ex Parte Merryman—an opinion of a single justice rather than a decision of the Court, be it noted. Merryman was released from Fort McHenry and transferred to civil authority. Although his treasonable activities were notorious, the case against him was dropped. This inconclusive outcome of the case left obscure the question of the President's right to suspend the writ of habeas corpus.*

✓          ✓          ✓

TANEY, C. J. The application in this case for a writ of *habeas corpus* is made to me under the 14th section of the Judiciary Act of 1789, which renders effectual for the citizen the constitutional privilege of the writ of *habeas corpus*. That act gives to the Courts of the United States, as well as to each justice of the Supreme Court, and to every District Judge, power to grant writs of *habeas corpus* for the purpose of an inquiry into the cause of commitment. The petition was presented to me at Washington, under the impression that I would order the prisoner to be brought before me there, but as he was

* 17 Federal Cases, 144.

confined in Fort McHenry, at the City of Baltimore, which is in my circuit, I resolved to hear it in the latter city, as obedience to the writ, under such circumstances, would not withdraw Gen. Cadwalader who had him in charge from the limits of his military command. . . .

A copy of the warrant or order, under which the prisoner was arrested, was demanded by his counsel, and refused. And it is not alleged in the return that any specific act, constituting an offence against the laws of the United States, has been charged against him upon oath; but he appears to have been arrested upon general charges of treason and rebellion, without proof, and without giving the names of the witnesses, or specifying the acts, which in the judgement of the military officer, constituted the crime. And having the prisoner thus in custody on these vague and unsupported accusations, he refuses to obey the writ of *habeas corpus,* upon the ground that he is duly authorized by the President to suspend it.

The case, then, is simply this: A military officer residing in Pennsylvania issues an order to arrest a citizen of Maryland, upon vague and indefinite charges, without any proof, so far as appears. Under this order his house is entered in the night; he is seized as a prisoner, and conveyed to Fort McHenry, and there kept in close confinement. And when a *habeas corpus* is served on the commanding officer, requiring him to produce the prisoner before a justice of the Supreme Court, in order that he may examine into the legality of the imprisonment, the answer of the officer is that he is authorized by the President to suspend the writ of *habeas corpus* at his discretion, and, in the exercise of that discretion, suspends it in this case, and on that ground refuses obedience to the writ.

As the case comes before me, therefore, I understand that the President not only claims the right to suspend the writ of *habeas corpus* himself, at his discretion, but to delegate that discretionary power to a military officer, and to leave it to him to determine whether he will or will not obey judicial process that may be served upon him.

No official notice has been given to the Courts of Justice, or to the public, by proclamation or otherwise, that the President claimed this power and had exercised it in the matter stated in the return. And I certainly listened to it with some surprise, for I had supposed it to be one of those points of constitutional law upon which there was no difference of opinion, and that it was admitted on all hands that the privilege of the writ could not be suspended except by act of Congress. . . .

The clause in the Constitution which authorizes the suspension of the privilege of the writ of *habeas corpus* is in the ninth section of the first article.

This article is devoted to the Legislative Department of the United States, and has not the slightest reference to the Executive Department. . . .

The power of legislation granted by this latter clause is by its word carefully confined to the specific objects before enumerated. But as this limitation was unavoidably somewhat indefinite, it was deemed necessary to guard more effectively certain great cardinal principles essential to the liberty of the citizen and to the rights and equality of the States by denying to Congress, in express terms, any power of legislation over them. It was apprehended, it seems, that such legislation might be attempted under the pretext that it was necessary and proper to carry into execution the powers granted; and it was determined that there should be no room to doubt, where rights of such vital importance were concerned, and accordingly this clause is immediately followed by an enumeration of certain subjects to which the powers of legislation shall not extend; and the great importance which the framers of the Constitution attached to the privilege of the writ of *habeas corpus* to protect the liberty of the citizen, is proved by the fact that its suspension, except in cases of invasion and rebellion, is first in the list of prohibited power; and even in these cases the power is denied and its exercise prohibited unless the public safety shall require it. It is true that in the cases mentioned Congress is of necessity to judge whether the public safety does or does not require it; and its judgement is conclusive. But the introduction of these words is a standing admonition to the legislative body of the danger of suspending it and of the extreme caution they should exercise before they give the Government of the United States such power over the liberty of a citizen.

It is the second Article of the Constitution that provides for the organization of the Executive Department, and enumerates the powers conferred on it, and prescribes its duties. And if the high power over the liberty of the citizens now claimed was intended to be conferred on the President, it would undoubtedly be found in plain words in this article. But there is not a word in it that can furnish the slightest ground to justify the exercise of the power. . . .

With such provisions in the Constitution, expressed in language too clear to be misunderstood by anyone, I can see no ground whatever for supposing that the President in any emergency or in any state of things can authorize the suspension of the privilege of the writ of *habeas corpus,* or arrest a citizen except in aid of the judicial power. He certainly does not faithfully execute the laws if he takes upon himself legislative power by suspending the writ of *habeas corpus*—and the judicial power, also, by arresting and imprisoning a person without due process of law. Nor can any argument be drawn from the nature of sovereignty, or the necessities of government for self-defence, in times of tumult and danger. The Government of the United States is one of delegated and limited powers. It derives its existence and authority altogether from the Constitution, and neither of its branches—executive, legislative, or judicial—can exercise any of the powers of government beyond those specified and granted. . . .

To guide me to a right conclusion, I have the Commentaries on the Constitution of the United States of the late Mr. Justice Story . . . and also the clear and authoritative decision of (the Supreme) Court, given more than a half century since, and conclusively establishing the principles I have above stated. Mr. Story, speaking in his Commentaries of the *habeas corpus* clause in the Constitution, says:

"It is obvious that cases of a peculiar emergency may arise, which may justify, nay, even require, the temporary suspension of any right to the writ. . . . Hitherto no suspension of the writ has ever been authorized by Congress since the establishment of the Constitution. It would seem, as the power is given to Congress to suspend the writ of *habeas corpus* in cases of rebellion or invasion, that the right to judge whether the exigency had arisen must exclusively belong to that body". *Commentaries,* section 1,336.

And Chief Justice Marshall, in delivering the opinion of the Supreme Court in the case *ex parte* Bollman and

Swartwout, uses this decisive language, in 4 Cranch, 101:

"If at any time the public safety should require the suspension of the powers vested by this act in the courts of the United States, it is for the Legislature to say so. That question depends on political considerations, on which the Legislature is to decide. Until the legislative will be expressed, this court can only see its duty, and must obey the laws."

I can add nothing to these clear and emphatic words of my great predecessor.

But the documents before me show that the military authority in this case has gone far beyond the mere suspension of the privilege of the writ of *habeas corpus*. It has, by force of arms, thrust aside the judicial authorities and officers to whom the Constitution has confided the power and duty of interpreting and administering the laws, and substituted a military government in its place, to be administered and executed by military officers. . . .

The Constitution provides, as I have before said, that "no person shall be deprived of life, liberty, or property without due process of law". It declares that "the right of the people to be secure in their persons, houses, papers, and effects against unreasonable searches and seizures shall not be violated, and no warrant shall issue but upon probable cause, supported by oath or affirmation, and particularly describing the place to be searched and the persons or things to be seized." It provides that the party accused shall be entitled to a speedy trial in a court of justice.

And these great and fundamental laws, which Congress itself could not suspend, have been disregarded and suspended, like the writ of *habeas corpus,* by a military order, supported by force of arms. Such is the case now before me; and I can only say that if the authority which the Constitution has confided to the judiciary department and judicial officers may thus upon any pretext or under any circumstances be usurped by the military power at its discretion, the people of the United States are no longer living under a Government of laws, but every citizen holds life, liberty, and property at the will and pleasure of the army officer in whose military district he may happen to be found.

In such a case my duty was too plain to be mistaken. I have exercised all the power which the Constitution and laws confer on me, but that power has been resisted by a force too strong for me to overcome. It is possible that the officer who had incurred this grave responsibility may have misunderstood his instructions, and exceeded the authority intended to be given him. I shall therefore order all the proceedings in this case, with my opinion, to be filed and recorded in the Circuit Court of the United States for the District of Maryland, and direct the clerk to transmit a copy . . . to the President of the United States. It will then remain for that high officer, in fulfillment of his constitutional obligation to "take care that the laws be faithfully executed" to determine what measure he will take to cause the civil process of the United States to be respected and enforced.

# — 31 —

# EX PARTE MILLIGAN, 1866*

*To settle the vexatious problem of the suspension of the writ of habeas corpus, Congress authorized the President to suspend it by an act of March 3, 1863. Under this authority, on September 15, 1863, Lincoln suspended the writ in cases where officers held persons for offenses against the military service. It was in these circumstances that Lambdin Milligan, one of the most notorious Copperheads in Indiana, was arrested by the military authorities and charged with disloyal practices. Tried by a military commission, Milligan was found guilty of fomenting rebellion and sentenced to be hanged. He petitioned the civil court for a writ of habeas corpus and after the War the case went to the Supreme Court of the United States. The decision of the Court, rendered by Lincoln's friend Justice Davis, is one of the most notable in our history. It is an eloquent reassertion of the principle of the superiority of the civil over the military and has long remained a landmark of our constitutional history. Not only*

* U. S. Supreme Court Reports, 4 Wallace, 2.

*did it condemn military tribunals where the civil courts were open but, by implication, raised serious doubts as to the legality of congressional reconstruction. Four judges, including the Chief Justice, concurred with the result but differed with the Court on the interpretation of congressional authority.*

✔          ✔          ✔

DAVIS, J. . . . The importance of the main question presented by this record cannot be overstated; for it involves the very framework of the government and the fundamental principles of American liberty.

During the late wicked rebellion, the temper of the times did not allow that calmness in deliberation and discussion so necessary to a correct conclusion of a purely judicial question. *Then,* considerations of safety were mingled with the exercise of power; and feelings and interests prevailed which are happily terminated. *Now,* that the public safety is assured, this question, as well as all others, can be discussed and decided without passion or the admixture of any element not required to form a legal judgment. We approach the investigation of this case, fully sensible of the magnitude of the inquiry and the necessity of full and cautious deliberation. . . .

The controlling question in the case is this: Upon the *facts* stated in Milligan's petition, and the exhibits filed, had the military commission mentioned in it *jurisdiction,* legally, to try and sentence him? Milligan, not a resident of one of the rebellious states, or a prisoner of war, but a citizen of Indiana for twenty years past, and never in the military or naval service, is, while at his home, arrested by the military power of the United States, imprisoned, and, on certain criminal charges preferred against him, tried, convicted, and sentenced to be hanged by a military commission, organized under the direction of the military commander of the military district of Indiana. Had this tribunal the legal power and authority to try and punish this man?

No graver question was ever considered by this court, nor one which more nearly concerns the rights of the whole people; for it is the birthright of every American citizen when charged with crime, to be tried and punished according to law. The power of punishment is alone through the means which the laws have provided for that purpose, and if they are ineffectual, there is an immunity from punishment no matter how great an offender the individual may be, or how much his crimes may have shocked the sense of justice of the country, or endangered its safety. By the protection of the law human rights are secured; withdraw that protection, and they are at the mercy of wicked rulers, or the clamor of an excited people. If there was law to justify this military trial, it is not our province to interfere; if there was not, it is our duty to declare the nullity of the whole proceedings. The decision of this question does not depend on argument or judicial precedents, numerous and highly illustrative as they are. These precedents inform us of the extent of the struggle to preserve liberty, and to relieve those in civil life from military trials. The founders of our government were familiar with the history of that struggle, and secured in a written Constitution every right which the people had wrested from power during a contest of ages. By that Constitution and the laws authorized by it this question must be determined. The provisions of that instrument on the administration of criminal justice are too plain and direct to leave room for misconstruction or doubt of their true meaning. Those applicable to this case are found in that clause of the original Constitution which says, "That the trial of all crimes, except in case of impeachment, shall be by jury"; and in the fourth, fifth, and sixth articles of the amendments. . . .

Time has proven the discernment of our ancestors; for even these provisions, expressed in such plain English words, that it would seem the ingenuity of man could not evade them, are *now,* after the lapse of more than seventy years, sought to be avoided. . . . The Constitution of the United States is a law for rulers and people, equally in war and in peace, and covers with the shield of its protection all classes of men, at all times, and under all circumstances. No doctrine involving more pernicious consequences was ever invented by the wit of man than that any of its provisions can be suspended during any of the great exigencies of government. Such a doctrine leads directly to anarchy or despotism, but the theory of necessity on which it is based is false; for the government, within the Constitution, has all the powers granted to it which are necessary to preserve its existence; as has been happily proved by the result of the great effort to throw off its just authority.

Have any of the rights guaranteed by the Constitution been violated in the case of Milligan? and if so, what are they?

Every trial involves the exercise of judicial power; and from what source did the military commission that tried him derive their authority? Certainly no part of the judicial power of the country was conferred on them; because the Constitution expressly vests it "in one Supreme Court and such inferior courts as the Congress may from time to time ordain and establish," and it is not pretended that the commission was a court ordained and established by Congress. They cannot justify on the mandate of the President, because he is controlled by law, and has his appropriate sphere of duty, which is to execute, not to make, the laws; and there is "no unwritten criminal code to which resort can be had as a source of jurisdiction."

But it is said that the jurisdiction is complete under the "laws and usages of war."

It can serve no useful purpose to inquire what those laws and usages are, whence they originated, where found, and on whom they operate; they can never be applied to citizens in states which have upheld the authority of the government, and where the courts are open and their process unobstructed. This court has judicial knowledge that in Indiana the federal authority was always unopposed, and its courts always open to hear criminal accusations and redress grievances; and no usage of war could sanction a military trial there for any offense whatever of a citizen in civil life, in nowise connected with the military service. Congress could grant no such power; and to the honor of our national legislature be it said, it has never been provoked by the state of the country even to attempt its exercise. One of the plainest constitutional provisions was, therefore, infringed when Milligan was tried by a court not ordained and established by Congress, and not composed of judges appointed during good behavior.

Why was he not delivered to the circuit court of Indiana to be proceeded against according to law? No reason of necessity could be urged against it; because Congress had declared penalties against the offenses charged, provided for their punishment, and directed that court to hear and determine them. And soon after this military tribunal was ended, the circuit court met, peacefully transacted its business, and adjourned. It needed no bayonets to protect it, and required no military aid to execute its judgments. It was held in a state, eminently distinguished for patriotism, by judges commissioned during the rebellion who were provided with juries, upright, intelligent, and selected by a marshal appointed by the President. The government had no right to conclude that Milligan, if guilty, would not receive in that court merited punishment; for its records disclose that it was constantly engaged in the trial of similar offenses, and was never interrupted in its administration of criminal justice. If it was dangerous, in the distracted condition of affairs, to leave Milligan unrestrained of his liberty, because he "conspired against the government, afforded aid and comfort to rebels, and incited the people to insurrection," the *law* said, arrest him, confine him closely, render him powerless to do further mischief; and then present his case to the grand jury of the district, with proofs of his guilt, and, if indicted, try him according to the course of the common law. If this had been done, the Constitution would have been vindicated, the law of 1863 enforced, and the securities for personal liberty preserved and defended.

Another guarantee of freedom was broken when Milligan was denied a trial by jury. The great minds of the country have differed on the correct interpretation to be given to the various provisions of the federal Constitution; and judicial decision has been often invoked to settle their true meaning; but until recently no one ever doubted that the right of trial by jury was forfeited in the organic law against the power of attack. It is *now* assailed; but if ideas can be expressed in words, and language has any meaning, *this right*—one of the most valuable in a free country—is preserved to every one accused of crime who is not attached to the army, or navy, or militia in actual service. . . .

It is claimed that martial law covers with its broad mantle the proceedings of this military commission. The proposition is this: that in a time of war the commander of an armed force (if, in his opinion, the exigencies of, the country demand it, and of which he is to judge) has the power, within the lines of his military district, to suspend all civil rights and their remedies, and subject citizens as well as soldiers to the rule of *his will;* and in the exercise of his lawful authority cannot be restrained, except by his superior officer or the President of the United States.

If this position is sound to the extent claimed, then when war exists, foreign or domestic, and the country is subdivided into military departments for mere convenience, the commander of one of them can, if he chooses, within his limits, on the plea of necessity, with the approval of the Executive, substitute military force for, and to the exclusion of, the laws, and punish all persons, as he thinks right and proper, without fixed or certain rules.

The statement of this proposition shows its importance; for, if true, republican government is a failure, and there is an end of liberty regulated by law. Martial law, established on such a basis, destroys every guarantee of the Constitution, and effectually renders the "military independent of, and superior to, the civil power,"—the attempt to do which by the king of Great Britain was deemed by our fathers such an offense, that they assigned it to the world as one of the causes which impelled them to declare their independence. Civil liberty and this kind of martial law cannot endure together; the antagonism is irreconcilable; and, in the conflict, one or the other must perish.

This nation, as experience has proved, cannot always remain at peace, and has no right to expect that it will always have wise and humane rulers, sincerely attached to the principles of the Constitution. Wicked men, ambitious of power, with hatred of liberty and contempt of law, may fill the place once occupied by Washington and Lincoln; and if this right is conceded, and the calamities of war again befall us, the dangers to human liberty are frightful to contemplate. If our fathers had failed to provide for just such a contingency, they would have been false to the trust reposed in them. They knew—the history of the world told them—the nation they were founding, be its existence short or long, would be involved in war; how often or how long continued, human foresight could not tell; and that unlimited power, wherever lodged at such a time, was especially hazardous to freemen. For this, and other equally weighty reasons, they secured the inheritance they had fought to maintain, by incorporating in a written Constitution the safeguards which time had proved were essential to its preservation. Not one of these safeguards can the President, or Congress, or the judiciary disturb, except the one concerning the writ of habeas corpus.

It is essential to the safety of every government that, in a great crisis like the one we have just passed through, there should be a power somewhere of suspending the writ of habeas corpus. In every war, there are men of previously good character, wicked enough to counsel their fellow-citizens to resist the measures deemed necessary by a good government to sustain its just authority and overthrow its enemies; and their influence may lead to dangerous combinations. In the emergency of the times, an immediate public investigation according to law may not be possible; and yet the peril to the country may be too imminent to suffer such persons to go at large. Unquestionably, there is then an exigency which demands that the government, if it should see fit, in the exercise of a proper discretion, to make arrests, should not be required to produce the persons arrested in answer to a writ of habeas corpus. The Constitution goes no further. It does not say after a writ of habeas corpus is denied a citizen, that he shall be tried otherwise than by the course of the common law; if it had intended this result, it was easy by the use of direct words to have accomplished it. The illustrious men who framed that instrument were guarding the foundations of civil liberty against the abuses of unlimited power; they were full of wisdom, and the lessons of history informed them that a trial by an established court, assisted by an impartial jury, was the only sure way of protecting the citizen against oppression and wrong. Knowing this, they limited the suspension to one great right, and left the rest to remain forever inviolable. But, it is insisted that the safety of the country in time of war demands that this broad claim for martial law shall be sustained. If this were true, it could be well said that a country, preserved at the sacrifice of all the cardinal principles of liberty, is not worth the cost of preservation. Happily, it is not so.

It will be borne in mind that this is not a question of the power to proclaim martial law, when war exists in a community and the courts and civil authorities are over-thrown. Nor is it a question what rule a military commander, at the head of his army, can impose on states in rebellion to cripple their resources and quell the insurrection. The jurisdcition claimed is much more extensive. The necessities of the service, during the late rebellion, required that the loyal states should be placed within the limits of certain military districts and commanders appointed in them; and, it is urged, that this, in a military sense, constituted them the theatre of military operations; and, as in this case, Indiana had been and was again threatened with invasion by the enemy, the occasion was furnished to establish martial law. The conclusion does not follow from the premises. If armies were collected in Indiana, they were to be employed in another locality, where the laws were obstructed and the national authority disputed. On *her* soil there was no hostile foot; if once invaded, that invasion was at an end, and with it all pretext for martial law. Martial law cannot arise from a *threatened* invasion. The necessity must be actual and present; the invasion real, such as effectually closes the courts and deposes the civil administration.

It is difficult to see how the *safety* of the country required martial law in Indiana. If any of her citizens were plotting treason, the power of arrest could secure them, until the government was prepared for their trial, when the courts were open and ready to try them. It was as easy to protect witnesses before a civil as a military tribunal; and as there could be no wish to convict, except on sufficient legal evidence, surely an ordained and established court was better able to judge of this than a military tribunal composed of gentlemen not trained to the profession of the law.

It follows, from what has been said on this subject, that there are occasions when martial rule can be properly applied. If, in foreign invasion or civil war, the courts are actually closed, and it is impossible to administer criminal justice according to law, *then,* on the theatre of active military operations, where war really prevails, there is a necessity to furnish a substitute for the civil authority, thus overthrown, to preserve the safety of the army and society; and as no power is left but the military, it is allowed to govern by martial rule until the laws can have their free course. As necessity creates the rule, so it limits

its duration; for, if this government is continued *after* the courts are reinstated, it is a gross usurpation of power. Martial rule can never exist where the courts are open, and in the proper and unobstructed exercise of their juris-diction. It is also confined to the locality of actual war. Because, during the late rebellion it could have been enforced in Virginia, where the national authority was overturned and the courts driven out, it does not follow that it should obtain in Indiana, where that authority was never disputed, and justice was always administered. . . .

— 32 —

# A SOUTHERN UNIONIST: JAMES LOUIS PETIGRU, 1863 *

*Unionist sentiment was weaker in South Carolina than in any other Southern state and probably weaker in Charleston than in any other city.*

*This epitaph on the Petigru monument in St. Michael's churchyard, Charleston, is evidence of the respect in which the wartime South held honest difference of opinion. A lawyer and a public servant, James Petigru was probably the most distinguished of South Carolina Unionists. The toleration accorded him was in part a product of the sophistication of Charleston, in part the class consciousness which accepted eccentricity in its aristocracy, in part the respect for intellectual independence more common in the Civil War generation than in our own.*

✓          ✓          ✓

* James Petigru Carson, *Life, Letters and Speeches of James Louis Petigru, The Union Man of South Carolina* (Washington, D. C., 1920), p. 487.

## JAMES LOUIS PETIGRU

Born at
Abbeville May 10th 1789
Died at Charleston March 9th 1863

JURIST. ORATOR. STATESMAN. PATRIOT.

Future times will hardly know how great a life
This simple stone commemorates—
The tradition of his Eloquence, his
Wisdom and his Wit may fade:
But he lived for ends more durable than fame,
His Eloquence was the protection of the poor and wronged;
His Learning illuminated the principles of Law—
In the admiration of his Peers,
In the respect of his People,
In the affection of his Family
His was the highest place;
The just meed
Of his kindness and forbearance
His dignity and simplicity
His brilliant genius and his unwearied industry
Unawed by Opinion,
Unseduced by Flattery,
Undismayed by Disaster,
He confronted Life with antique Courage
And Death with Christian Hope.


In the great Civil War
He withstood his People for his Country
But his People did homage to the Man
Who held his conscience higher than their praise
And his Country
Heaped her honors on the grave of the Patriot,
To whom living,
His own righteous self-respect sufficed
Alike for Motive and Reward.


"Nothing is here for tears, nothing to wail,
Or knock the breast; no weakness, no contempt,
Dispraise or blame; nothing but well and fair
And what may quiet us in a life so noble."

# — 33 —

# DISCONTENT IN THE CONFEDERACY

## A. Joseph E. Brown to Alexander H. Stephens, September 1, 1862*

*Neither the North nor the South was wholly united during the War; it is interesting that desertion from both the Union and Confederate armies ran to about ten percent. Lincoln had to deal with discontent caused by war weariness and apathy as well as draft riots and Copperheadism to out-and-out treason. So too did Davis. If Lincoln had his Seymours and Vallandighams, Davis was burdened with men like Governor Brown of Georgia and Governor Vance of North Carolina. Part of Southern discontent was inspired by a sincere, although narrow and doctrinaire, devotion to states rights, part by personal hostility to President Davis, part by dissatisfaction with the conduct of the War, and an increasingly large part by sheer war weariness and defeatism. State-righters, like Governors Brown and Vance and Vice-President Stephens, thought the tyranny of Richmond was worse than that of Washington and were particularly outraged by conscription and the suspension of the writ of habeas corpus. Nowhere was discontent more ardent or more effective than in Georgia. We present here a letter from the egregious Governor Brown, the most powerful of all the state governors and the one who, by his policy of putting the interest of Georgia first, effectively sabotaged the Confederacy.*

✓        ✓        ✓

* Ulrich B. Phillips, ed., "The Correspondence of Robert Toombs, Alexander H. Stephens, and Howell Cobb," in the *Annual Report of the American Historical Association*, 1911 (Washington, D. C., 1913), Vol. II, pp. 605-606.

(*Private*)

CANTON [GEORGIA], Sept. 1st, 1862

DEAR SIR: I have the pleasure to acknowledge the receipt of your letter of the 26th ult. and am gratified that you take the view which you have expressed about the action of Genl. Bragg in his declaration of martial law over Atlanta and his appoint[ment], as the newspapers say, of a civil governor with aids, etc.

I have viewed this proceeding as I have others of our military authorities of late with painful apprehensiveness for the future. It seems military men are assuming the whole powers of government to themselves and setting at defiance constitutions, laws, state rights, state sovereignty, and every other principle of civil liberty, and that our people engrossed in the struggle with the enemy are disposed to submit to these bold usurpations tending to military despotism without murmur, much less resistance. I should have called this proceeding into question before this time but I was hopeful from the indications which I had noted that Congress would take such action as would check these dangerous usurpations of power, and for the further reasons that I have already come almost into conflict with the Confederate authorities in vindication of what I have considered the rights of the State and people of Georgia, and I was fearful, as no other governor seems to raise these questions, that I might be considered by good and true men in and out of Congress too refractory for the times. I had therefore concluded to take no notice of this matter till the meeting of the legislature when I expect to ask the representatives of the people to define the bounds to which they desire the Governor to go in the defense of the rights and sovereignty of the state. I confess I have apprehensions that our present General Assembly does not properly reflect the sentiments of our people upon this great question, but if the Executive goes beyond the bounds where he is sustained by the representatives of the people he exposes himself to censure without the moral power to do service to the great principles involved. I fear we have much more to apprehend from military despotism than from subjugation by the enemy. I trust our generals will improve well their time while we have the advantage and the enemy are organizing another army. Hoping that your health is good and begging that you will write me when your important duties are not too pressing to permit it, I am very truly your friend.

## B. Jonathan Worth to Jesse G. Henshaw, August 24, 1863*

*North Carolina presented a special case. Never as deeply committed to slavery as her affluent neighbors to the North and the South, she might very well have refused to secede had it not been for her geographical position. Although North Carolina contributed her full share to the War and perhaps somewhat more than her full quota of men, war weariness and defeatism early found support in the mountainous regions of the western part of the state.*

*Jonathan Worth was an old-line Whig politician who fought nullification in the 1830's and secession in 1861 but—like so many others—went with his state when the crisis materialized. During the war he was State Treasurer of North Carolina; in 1865 he was elected to the governorship and re-elected the following year.*

✓          ✓          ✓

RALEIGH, Aug. 24, 1863

I hardly know whether I am in favor of the peace meetings or not. On the one hand, it is very certain that the President and his advisers will not make peace, if not forced into it by the masses and the privates in the army. Their cry echoed by almost every press is: "Independence, or the last man and the last dollar." The North will not make peace on the basis of Independence. The real question which nobody—not even Holden—will squarely present is, shall we fight on with certain desolation and impoverishment and probable ultimate defeat; or make peace on the basis of reconstruction? Nearly every public man —every journal, political and religious, and every politician, in the fervor of their patriotism, has vociferously declared in favor of "the last man and the last dollar" cry. These classes cannot be consistent unless they still cry war. Many believe the masses in their saner hours never approved the war and would rather compromise on

* J. G. de Roulhac Hamilton, ed., *The Correspondence of Jonathan Worth* (Raleigh, North Carolina, 1909), Vol. I, pp. 257-258.

the basis of the Constitution of the U. S. with such additional securities against any future rupture as could be
agreed on. If there be any sense in peace meetings they
mean reconstruction. They may rather do mischief if they
are not so imposing as to force the administration to reconstruction. They will be impotent and mischievous if
the army is still for war to the last man and the last
dollar. I do not know the sentiments of the rank and file
of the army.

I am for peace on almost any terms and fear we shall
never have it until the Yankees dictate it. Upon the whole
I would not go into a peace meeting now or advise others
to go into one, particularly in Randolph—but I have no
repugnance to them in other places and see no other
chance to get to an early end of this wicked war, but by
the action of the masses who have the fighting to do. If
an open rupture occur between Gov. V[ance] and Mr.
Holden, it will be ruinous to us. There ought to be none
and I trust there will be none. There is no difference
between them that justifies a breach. The Governor con-
cedes the right of the people to hold meetings and express
their wishes, but he deems such meetings inexpedient and
tending to dissatisfaction and disorganization in the army
and that no honorable peace can be made, after we cease
to present a strong military front. The Gov. acts consistently and in the eminent difficult position he occupied, I
doubt whether any pilot could manage the crippled ship
in such a storm with more skill. Repress all expressions
of dissatisfaction against him. He values the extravagant
eulogiums of the fire-eaters at their worth. They are playing an adroit game. They would get up dissention between the Gov. and Holden and then break up the Con-
servative party and seize the helm of Government.

## — 34 —

# WARTIME LEGISLATION

*The military, political, and diplomatic conduct of the War loomed so large that we sometimes forget that life —and politics—went on in the North almost as usual. The withdrawal of Southern Democrats from the halls of Congress made it possible for the Republicans—with the assistance, to be sure, of some of the Northern Democrats—to push through a large part of their program. We give here excerpts from three historic pieces of legislation enacted by the wartime Congress.*

### A. Homestead Act, May 20, 1862*

*A Homestead Act had passed both houses of Congress in 1859 only to be vetoed by President Buchanan. With the success of the Republican Party in 1860, homestead legislation was assured. The Homestead Act brought to an end one period of American land policy and inaugurated a new policy which, with modifications, has been followed since 1862.*

*An Act to secure homesteads to actual settlers on the public domain.*

*Be it enacted,* That any person who is the head of a family, or who has arrived at the age of twenty-one years, and is a citizen of the United States, or who shall have filed his declaration of intention to become such, as required by the naturalization laws of the United States, and who has never borne arms against the United States Government or given aid and comfort to its enemies, shall, from and after the first of January, eighteen hundred and sixty-three, be entitled to enter one quarter-section or a

* *U. S. Statutes at Large,* Vol. XII, pp. 392 ff.

less quantity of unappropriated public lands, upon which said person may have filed a pre-emption claim, or which may, at the time the application is made, be subject to pre-emption at one dollar and twenty-five cents, or less, per acre; or eighty acres or less of such unappropriated lands, at two dollars and fifty cents per acre, to be located in a body, in conformity to the legal subdivisions of the public lands, and after the same shall have been surveyed: *Provided,* That any person owning or residing on land may, under the provisions of this act, enter other land lying contiguous to his or her said land, which shall not, with the land so already owned and occupied, exceed in the aggregate one hundred and sixty acres.

Sec. 2. That the person applying for the benefit of this act shall, upon application to the register of the land office in which he or she is about to make such entry, make affidavit before the said register or receiver that he or she is the head of a family, or is twenty-one or more years of age, or shall have performed service in the Army or Navy of the United States, and that he has never borne arms against the Government of the United States or given aid and comfort to its enemies, and that such application is made for his or her exclusive use and benefit, and that said entry is made for the purpose of actual settlement and cultivation, and not, either directly or indirectly, for the use or benefit of any other person or persons whomsoever; and upon filing the said affidavit with the register or receiver, and on payment of ten dollars, he or she shall thereupon be permitted to enter the quantity of land specified: *Provided, however,* That no certificate shall be given or patent issued therefor until the expiration of five years from the date of such entry; and if, at the expiration of such time, or at any time within two years thereafter, the person making such entry—or if he be dead, his widow; or in case of her death, his heirs or devisee; or in case of a widow making such entry, her heirs or devisee, in case of her death—shall prove by two credible witnesses that he, she, or they have resided upon or cultivated the same for the term of five years immediately succeeding the time of filing the affidavit aforesaid, and shall make affidavit that no part of said land has been alienated, and that he has borne true allegiance to the Government of the United States; then, in such case, he, she, or they, if at that time a citizen of the United

States, shall be entitled to a patent, as in other cases provided for by law: *And provided, further,* That in case of the death of both father and mother, leaving an infant child or children under twenty-one years of age, the right and fee shall inure to the benefit of said infant child or children; and the executor, administrator, or guardian may, at any time within two years after the death of the surviving parent, and in accordance with the laws of the State in which such children for the time being have their domicile, sell said land for the benefit of said infants, but for no other purpose; and the purchaser shall acquire the absolute title by the purchase, and be entitled to a patent from the United States, on payment of the office fees and sum of money herein specified. . . .

### B. Pacific Railway Act, July 1, 1862*

*The idea of a transcontinental railroad had been broached in the 1840's, and the rapid growth of California after 1849 brought it sharply to the attention of the country. Throughout the 1850's there was a general acquiescence in the idea that the road was necessary, but sectional rivalries prevented any agreement on the route which the road should take. In 1853 Congress authorized a survey of various routes, and its responsibility was assumed under the direction of Secretary of War Davis. The secession of the Southern States cleared the way for a northern route, and in 1862 the first Pacific Railway Bill, authorizing the transcontinental railroad and granting generous government aid, was passed. Two years later a second Pacific Railway Act doubled the land grants and provided that the government have a second instead of a first mortgage on the railroad property.*

✓       ✓       ✓

*An Act to aid in the Construction of a Railroad and Telegraph Line from the Missouri River to the Pacific Ocean. . . .*

*Be it enacted,* That Walter S. Burgess [names of corporators]; together with five commissioners to be appointed by the Secretary of the Interior . . . are hereby created and erected into a body corporate . . . by the name . . . of "The Union Pacific Railroad Company"

* *U. S. Statutes at Large,* Vol. XII, pp. 489 ff.

. . . ; and the said corporation is hereby authorized and empowered to lay out, locate, construct, furnish, maintain and enjoy a continuous railroad and telegraph . . . from a point on the one hundredth meridian of longitude west from Greenwich, between the south margin of the valley of the Republican River and the north margin of the valley of the Platte River, to the western boundary of Nevada Territory, upon the route and terms hereinafter provided. . . .

SEC. 2. That the right of way through the public lands be . . . granted to said company for the construction of said railroad and telegraph line; and the right . . . is hereby given to said company to take from the public lands adjacent to the line of said road, earth, stone, timber, and other materials for the construction thereof; said right of way is granted to said railroad to the extent of two hundred feet in width on each side of said railroad when it may pass over the public lands, including all necessary grounds for stations, buildings, workshops, and depots, machine shops, switches, side tracks, turn tables, and water stations. The United States shall extinguish as rapidly as may be the Indian titles to all lands falling under the operation of this act. . . .

SEC. 3. That there be . . . granted to the said company, for the purpose of aiding in the construction of said railroad and telegraph line, and to secure the safe and speedy transportation of mails, troops, munitions of war, and public stores thereon, every alternate section of public land, designated by odd numbers, to the amount of five alternate sections per mile on each side of said railroad, on the line thereof, and within the limits of ten miles on each side of said road. . . . *Provided* That all mineral lands shall be excepted from the operation of this act; but where the same shall contain timber, the timber thereon is hereby granted to said company. . . .

SEC. 5. That for the purposes herein mentioned the Secretary of the Treasury shall . . . in accordance with the provisions of this act, issue to said company bonds of the United States of one thousand dollars each, payable in thirty years after date, paying six per centum per annum interest . . . to the amount of sixteen of said bonds per mile for each section of forty miles; and to secure the repayment to the United States . . . of the amount of said bonds . . . the issue of said bonds . . . shall ipso facto constitute a first mortgage on the whole line of the railroad and telegraph. . . .

SEC. 9. That the Leavenworth, Pawnee and Western Railroad Company of Kansas are hereby authorized to construct a railroad and telegraph line . . . upon the same terms and conditions in all respects as are provided [for construction of the Union Pacific Railroad]. . . . The Central Pacific Railroad Company of California are hereby authorized to construct a railroad and telegraph line from the Pacific coast . . . to the eastern boundaries of California, upon the same terms and conditions in all respects [as are provided for the Union Pacific Railroad].

SEC. 10. . . . And the Central Pacific Railroad Company of California after completing its road across said State, is authorized to continue the construction of said railroad and telegraph through the Territories of the United States to the Missouri River . . . upon the terms and conditions provided in this act in relation to the Union Pacific Railroad Company, until said roads shall meet and connect. . . .

SEC. 11. That for three hundred miles of said road most mountainous and difficult of construction, to wit: one hundred and fifty miles westerly from the eastern base of the Rocky Mountains, and one hundred and fifty miles eastwardly from the western base of the Sierra Nevada mountains . . . the bonds to be issued to aid in the construction thereof shall be treble the number per mile hereinbefore provided . . . ; and between the sections last named of one hundred and fifty miles each, the bonds to be issued to aid in the construction thereof shall be double the number per mile first mentioned. . . .

## C. Morrill Act, July 2, 1862*

*This act granting public lands for the support of agricultural and industrial education is the most important piece of legislation on behalf of education passed by the Congress of the United States prior to 1963. Under the terms of this act, approximately 13 million acres of the public domain were given to the states for the establishment of mechanical and agricultural colleges or for the expansion of existing colleges and universities. The act gave a tremendous impetus to the movement for estab-*

* U. S. Statutes at Large, Vol. XII, p. 503.

*lishing state universities. The real "father" of the act was J. B. Turner of the University of Illinois, but the act quite properly bears the name of Justin S. Morrill of Vermont, who had introduced it first in 1857 and again in 1862.*

✓          ✓          ✓

*An Act donating Public Lands to the several States and Territories which may provide Colleges for the Benefit of Agriculture and the Mechanic Arts.*

*Be it enacted* by the Senate and House of Representatives of the United States of America in Congress assembled, That there be granted to the several States, for the purposes hereinafter mentioned, an amount of public land, to be apportioned to each State a quantity equal to thirty thousand acres for each senator and representative in Congress to which the States are respectively entitled by the apportionment under the census of eighteen hundred and sixty: Provided, That no mineral lands shall be selected or purchased under the provisions of this act.

SEC. 2. And be it further enacted, That the land aforesaid, after being surveyed, shall be apportioned to the several States in sections or subdivisions of sections, not less than one quarter of a section; and whenever there are public lands in a State subject to sale at private entry at one dollar and twenty-five cents per acre, the quantity to which said State shall be entitled shall be selected from such lands within the limits of such State, and the Secretary of the Interior is hereby directed to issue to each of the States in which there is not the quantity of public lands subject to sale at private entry at one dollar and twenty-five cents per acre; to which said State may be entitled under the provisions of this act, land scrip to the amount in acres for the deficiency of its distributive share: said scrip to be sold by said States and the proceeds thereof applied to the uses and purposes prescribed in this act, and for no other use or purpose whatsoever. . . .

SEC. 4. And be it further enacted, That all moneys derived from the sale of the lands aforesaid by the States to which the lands are apportioned, and from the sale of land scrip hereinbefore provided for, shall be invested in stocks of the United States, or of the States, or some other safe stocks, yielding not less than five per centum upon the par value of said stocks; and that the moneys so invested shall constitute a perpetual fund, the capital of which shall remain forever undiminished, (except so far as may be provided in section fifth of this act,) and the interest of which shall be inviolably appropriated, by each State which may take and claim the benefit of this act, to the endowment, support, and maintenance of at least one college where the leading object shall be, without excluding other scientific and classical studies, and including military tactics, to teach such branches of learning as are related to agriculture and mechanic arts, in such manner as the legislatures of the State may respectively prescribe, in order to promote the liberal and practical education of the industrial classes in the several pursuits and professions in life.

SEC. 5. . . . No State while in a condition of rebellion or insurrection against the government of the United States shall be entitled to the benefit of this Act. . . .

# Part V

## GRAND STRATEGY

# — 35 —

## CONFEDERATE STRATEGY, 1862

*It is impossible to give in this book any documents recording or illuminating the military history of the War; happily these are amply provided in many readily available collections. It is, however, appropriate to give some indication of what might be called the "grand strategy" of the Confederacy and of the Union, in so far as their governments or their generals did indeed have a "grand strategy."*

*The Confederacy was in a particularly awkward position. On the one hand, every moral and military consideration dictated a purely defensive strategy; on the other hand, the imperative necessity of winning foreign recognition required some evidence that the South could conduct a war which, while it could not conceivably conquer the North, might persuade it to give up fighting as a hopeless task. Not only this, the South was confronted with another dilemma. On the one hand, the War, if it were to be successful, had to be fought as a single enterprise, and its entire strategy dictated control by a central authority. On the other hand, the Confederacy was, by its very nature, dedicated to the principles of states rights and decentralization.*

*How illuminating it is that the South's greatest soldier, Robert Lee, was not made Commander in Chief of the Confederate Armies until February, 1865. There was a further difficulty whose interpretation is still controversial —that was the role of President Davis himself. Davis was, of course, a military man: he fancied himself a military strategist of the first order and interfered continually in the conduct of the war.*

*There are, unfortunately, very few documents which tell us about the South's grand strategy. We have selected two articles of some importance that provide or illuminate the background of the Antietam campaign.*

✓        ✓        ✓

## A. R. E. Lee to Jefferson Davis*

HEADQUARTERS, ALEXANDRIA & LEESBURG ROAD
Near DRANESVILLE, September 3, 1862

MR. PRESIDENT:

The present seems to be the most propitious time since the commencement of the war for the Confederate Army to enter Maryland. The two grand armies of the United States that have been operating in Virginia, though now united, are much weakened and demoralized. Their new levies, of which I understand sixty thousand men have already been posted in Washington, are not yet organized, and will take some time to prepare for the field. If it is ever desired to give material aid to Maryland and afford her an opportunity of throwing off the oppression to which she is now subject, this would seem the most favorable. After the enemy had disappeared from the vicinity of Fairfax Court House and taken the road to Alexandria & Washington, I did not think it would be advantageous to follow him farther. I had no intention of attacking him in his fortifications, and am not prepared to invest them. If I possessed the necessary munitions, I should be unable to supply provisions for the troops. I therefore determined while threatening the approaches to Washington, to draw the troops into Loudoun, where forage and some provisions can be obtained, menace their possession of the Shenandoah Valley, and if found practicable, to cross into Maryland.

The purpose, if discovered, will have the effect of carrying the enemy north of the Potomac, and if prevented, will not result in much evil. The army is not properly equipped for an invasion of an enemy's territory. It lacks much of the material of war, is feeble in transportation,

* Clifford Dowdey, ed., *The Wartime Papers of R. E. Lee* (Boston, 1961), pp. 292-294.

the animals being much reduced, and the men are poorly provided with clothes, and in thousands of instances are destitute of shoes. Still we cannot afford to be idle, and though weaker than our opponents in men and military equipments, must endeavor to harass, if we cannot destroy them. I am aware that the movement is attended with much risk, yet I do not consider success impossible, and shall endeavor to guard it from loss. As long as the army of the enemy are employed on this frontier I have no fears for the safety of Richmond, yet I earnestly recommend that advantage be taken of this period of comparative safety to place its defence, both by land and water, in the most perfect condition. A respectable force can be collected to defend its approaches by land, and the steamer *Richmond* I hope is now ready to clear the river of hostile vessels. Should Genl [Braxton] Bragg find it impracticable to operate to advantage on his present frontier, his army, after leaving sufficient garrisons, could be advantageously employed in opposing the overwhelming numbers which it seems to be the intention of the enemy now to concentrate in Virginia. I have already been told by prisoners that some of [General Don Carlos] Buell's cavalry have been joined to Genl Pope's army, and have reason to believe that the whole of McClellan's, the larger portions of Burnside's & Cox's and a portion of [General David] Hunter's, are united to it. What occasions me most concern is the fear of getting out of ammunition. I beg you will instruct the Ordnance Department to spare no pains in manufacturing a sufficient amount of the best kind, & to be particular in preparing that for the artillery, to provide three times as much of the long range ammunition as of that for smooth bore or short range guns.

The points to which I desire the ammunition to be forwarded will be made known to the Department in time. If the Quartermaster Department can furnish any shoes, it would be the greatest relief.

We have entered upon September, and the nights are becoming cool.

I have the honor to be with high respect, your ob't servant

R. E. LEE
*Genl*

**B. Jefferson Davis to Genl. R. E. Lee, Cmdg. &c., Genl. B. Bragg, Comdg. &c., Genl. E. K. Smith, Comdg. &c.***

(Probable date Sept. 7, 1862)

SIRS: It is deemed proper that you should in accordance with established usage announce by proclamation to the people of ———— the motives and purposes of your presence among them at the head of an invading army, and you are instructed in such proclamation to make known,—

1st. That the Confederate Government is waging this war solely for self-defence, that it has no design of conquest or any other purpose than to secure peace and the abandonment by the United States of its pretensions to govern a people who have never been their subjects and who prefer self-government to a Union with them.

2nd. That this Government at the very moment of its inauguration sent commissioners to Washington to treat for a peaceful adjustment of all differences, but that these commissioners were not received not even allowed to communicate the object of their mission, and that on a subsequent occasion a communication from the President of the Confederacy to President Lincoln remained without answer, although a reply was promised by General Scott into whose hands the communication was delivered.

3rd. That among the pretexts urged for continuance of the War is the assertion that the Confederate Government desires to deprive the United States of the free navigation of the Western Rivers although the truth is that the Confederate Congress by public act, prior to the commencement of the War, enacted that "the peaceful navigation of the Mississippi River is hereby declared free to the citizens of the States upon its borders, or upon the borders of its navigable tributaries"—a declaration to which this Government has always been and is still ready to adhere.

4th. That now at a juncture when our arms have been successful, we restrict ourselves to the same just and moderate demand, that we made at the darkest period of our reverses, the simple demand that the people of the United States should cease to war upon us and permit us

* *Jefferson Davis, Constitutionalist,* Dunbar Rowland, ed. (Jackson: Mississippi Department of Archives and History, 1923), Vol. V, pp. 338-339.

to pursue our own path to happiness, while they in peace pursue theirs.

5th. That we are debarred from the renewal of formal proposals for peace by having no reason to expect that they would be received with the respect mutually due by nations in their intercourse, whether in peace or in war.

6th. That under these circumstances we are driven to protect our own country by transferring the seat of war to that of an enemy who pursues us with a relentless and apparently aimless hostility: That our fields have been laid waste, our people killed, many homes made desolate, and that rapine and murder have ravaged our frontiers, that the sacred right of self defence demands that if such a war is to continue its consequences shall fall on those who persist in their refusal to make peace.

7th. That the Confederate army therefore comes to occupy the territory of their enemies and to make it the theatre of hostilities. That with the people of ————— themselves rests the power to put an end to this invasion of their homes, for if unable to prevail on the Government of the United States to conclude a general peace, their own State Government in the exercise of its sovereignty can secure immunity from the desolating effects of warfare on the soil of the State by a separate treaty of peace which this Government will ever be ready to conclude on the most just and liberal basis.

8th. That the responsibility thus rests on the people of ————— of continuing an unjust and aggressive warfare upon the Confederate States, a warfare which can never end in any other manner than that now proposed. With them is the option of preserving the blessings of peace, by the simple abandonment of the design of subjugating a people over whom no right of dominion has been ever conferred either by God or man.

JEFFN. DAVIS

## — 36 —

# HOW THE ARMY OF NORTHERN VIRGINIA GOT ITS ORDNANCE, 1863*

*Almost wholly without industries, and cut off from Europe by the blockade, the Confederacy had to get its arms and equipment as best it could. Some ordnance was seized when the Confederate states seceded; some was imported before the blockade became effective; some was smuggled in from the North; substantial quantities were captured from the enemy or "gleaned" on the battlefield.*

*Colonel William Allan, from whose reminiscences this excerpt is taken, was Chief of Ordnance of the Second Army Corps and author of an invaluable history of the campaign in the Shenandoah Valley and of the Army of Northern Virginia.*

✓          ✓          ✓

The troops at this time [1863] were armed in a heterogeneous fashion. Many of the men had smooth bore muskets, calibre .69. Others had rifled muskets, calibre .54; and others still had Springfield muskets, calibre .58. There were some other arms, as, for instance, some Belgian rifles, calibre .70, but the three kinds I have mentioned were the principal kinds in the hands of the infantry in January, 1863. We were all anxious to replace the smooth bores with rifles, and especially with calibre .58, which was the model the Confederate as well as the Federal Government had adopted. The battlefields of the preceding summer had enabled many commands to exchange their smooth bores for Springfield muskets, but as nine-

* Colonel William Allan, "Reminiscences of Field Ordnance Service with the Army of Northern Virginia—1863-'5," *Southern Historical Society Papers* (1886), Vol. XIV, pp. 138-145.

tenths of the arms in the Confederacy at the beginning of the war had been smooth bore muskets, it required time and patience to effect a complete re-arming. This was finally done in the Second corps at Chancellorsville, but in the winter of 1862-'63, there was often found in the same brigade the three kinds of arms above enumerated, and the same wagon often carried the three kinds of ammunition required. During this winter it was found difficult to obtain arms as fast as we needed them for the new men, and of course we were very glad to take what the department could furnish. Between the first of January and the first of May, General Jackson's corps grew from about twenty-three thousand muskets to thirty-three thousand. These ten thousand arms we obtained from Richmond in small quantities, and they were of different calibres, but the corps was fully armed when it went to Chancellorsville. After that battle the men all had muskets, calibre .58, and henceforth but one sort of ammunition was needed.

Our artillery armament was even more heterogeneous. Six-pounder guns, howitzers, some Napoleons, three-inch rifles, ten-pounder Parrotts, and a few twenty-pounder Parrotts were in our corps, besides, probably, some other odd pieces. I remember a Blakely gun or two and a Whitworth, the latter used both at Chancellorsville and Gettysburg. Our batteries had been greatly improved by a number of guns captured from the enemy. We especially valued the three-inch rifles, which became the favorite field piece. During the winter of 1862-'63, the artillery was first thoroughly organized under General Pendleton as chief. Batteries were detached from brigades, and were organized into battalions, containing four batteries, usually of four guns each. A number of these battalions were assigned to each corps under the chief of artillery of that corps, while a number of others constituted the general reserve, of which General Pendleton took immediate oversight. All that our supplies admitted was done to thoroughly equip these batteries during the winter, and they were ready for action when the campaign opened. A train of wagons was organized to carry the reserve ammunition for the artillery, and this was placed in charge of the artillery ordnance officer of the corps, and, besides this, there was a reserve train for the army under the direct orders of the chief ordnance officer of the army. . . .

Gleaning the battlefields was one of the important duties of the field ordnance officers. They were directed to
save everything which could be made of use. Of course
they took care of the good arms and good ammunition,
but they had to preserve no less carefully all damaged
arms, gun barrels, wasted ammunition, of which the lead
was the valuable consideration, bayonets, cartridge-boxes,
&c. After Chancellorsville and the gathering which had
been done during the battle, an ordnance officer of the
Second corps was sent to the field with power to call upon
a neighboring brigade for as large details as he wished,
and he spent a week in gathering the débris of the battle
and sending it to Guiney's Station or Hamilton's Crossing, whence it was shipped to Richmond. My recollec-
tion is that over twenty thousand stand of damaged arms
were sent in this way to the arsenal, besides a considerable
quantity of lead, &c. After the first day at Gettysburg the
battlefield was gleaned, and such material as we had
transportation for sent back. . . .

In the winter of 1864 it was impossible to obtain an
adequate quantity of horseshoes and nails from the ordnance department. The cavalry, which had been with
General Early during that fall, had seen severe service,
and it was absolutely necessary, in reference to the future, to procure in some way a supply of horseshoes and
nails during the winter. We had to depend upon ourselves. I determined to establish, if possible, twenty forges
in Waynesboro', Augusta county, Virginia, and have
blacksmiths detailed from the army to make shoes and
nails. We sent through the country and got such black-
smith tools as we were able to find. I think I got some,
too, from Richmond, from the ordnance department.
There was no difficulty in getting good blacksmiths out
of the army. A number of men were put to work, and
horseshoes and nails began to accumulate. We soon ran
out of iron, however, and found that the department at
Richmond could not fully supply our wants. There was a
fine lot of iron at Columbia furnace, near Mount Jackson,
which was at this time in the debatable ground between
the two armies. This iron was of fine quality, suitable for
casting cannon as well as any other purpose. The commander of the arsenal informed me that if I could manage
to get this to Richmond he would give me back in bars as
much as I needed for horseshoes and nails. Trains of

wagons were sent after it from Staunton, and these trains were protected by cavalry, which General Early sent for the purpose, and they returned in safety with the iron, which was promptly shipped to Richmond.

From this time forward our forges were fully supplied, and I think when Sheridan overhauled and dispersed our forces at Waynesboro', at the beginning of March, 1865, we had manufactured some twenty thousand pounds of horseshoes and nails. They were loaded upon the cars, which were gotten through the tunnel, but were captured by some of Sheridan's people at or near Greenwood depot.

# — 37 —

# LINCOLN APPOINTS HOOKER TO COMMAND THE ARMY, January 26, 1863 *

*After Fredericksburg, General Burnside prepared an order dismissing Hooker and three other general officers for what he considered incompetence. This he laid before Lincoln with the choice of accepting it or dismissing him. Inevitably, Lincoln relieved Burnside from command and —less inevitably—appointed Hooker to his place. A West Pointer, with experience in the Florida campaign and the Mexican War, Hooker had been appointed Brigadier General of volunteers in 1861 and had fought in the Peninsular and the Antietam campaigns. Like Pope he was given to boasting. "My plans are perfect," Hooker said shortly after his appointment to the top command. "May God have mercy on General Lee for I will have none." Lincoln, as this famous letter reveals, was not so sure.*

✦          ✦          ✦

* *The War of the Rebellion . . . Official Records.* Series 1, Vol. XL, p. 4.

EXECUTIVE MANSION, WASHINGTON, D. C.,
                                         January 26, 1863
Major-General HOOKER:

GENERAL: I have placed you at the head of the Army of the Potomac. Of course I have done this upon what appears to me to be sufficient reasons, and yet I think it best for you to know that there are some things in regard to which I am not quite satisfied with you. I believe you to be a brave and skillful soldier, which, of course, I like. I also believe you do not mix politics with your profession, in which you are right. You have confidence in yourself, which is a valuable, if not an indispensable, quality. You are ambitious, which, within reasonable bounds, does good rather than harm; but I think that during General Burnside's command of the army you have taken counsel of your ambition, and thwarted him as much as you could, in which you did a great wrong to the country and to a most meritorious and honorable brother officer. I have heard, in such a way as to believe it, of your recently saying that both the Army and the Government needed a dictator. Of course, it was not for this, but in spite of it, that I have given you the command. Only those generals who gain successes can set up dictators. What I now ask of you is military success, and I will risk the dictatorship. The Government will support you to the utmost of its ability, which is neither more nor less than it has done or will do for all commanders. I much fear that the spirit which you have aided to infuse into the army, of criticizing their commander and withholding confidence from him, will now turn upon you. I shall assist you as far as I can to put it down. Neither you nor Napoleon, if he were alive again, could get any good out of an army while such a spirit prevails in it. And now beware of rashness. Beware of rashness, but with energy and sleepless vigilance go forward and give us victories.

                                         Yours, very truly,
                                         A. LINCOLN

# — 38 —

# GENERAL LEE OFFERS TO RESIGN AFTER GETTYSBURG, August 8, 1863*

*"It is all my fault,"* said Lee, on the afternoon of the third day of Gettysburg. History does not agree with that verdict; the fault was rather in that combination of circumstances which required General Lee to perform an impossible feat with inadequate resources. But it was characteristic of Lee that he should shoulder the blame for the failure of the invasion. On August 8, Lee sent President Davis an offer to resign. In his reply Davis referred finely to those "achievements which will make you and your army the subject of history and object of the world's admiration for generations to come."

✓          ✓          ✓

CAMP ORANGE, *August 8, 1863*

His Excellency JEFFERSON DAVIS,
      *President of the Confederate States:*

MR. PRESIDENT: Your letters of July 28 and August 2 have been received, and I have waited for a leisure hour to reply, but I fear that will never come. I am extremely obliged to you for the attention given to the wants of this army, and the efforts made to supply them. Our absentees are returning, and I hope the earnest and beautiful appeal made to the country in your proclamation may stir up the virtue of the whole people, and that they may see their duty and perform it. Nothing is wanted but that their fortitude should equal their bravery to insure the success of our cause. We must expect reverses, even defeats. They are sent to teach us wisdom and prudence, to call

* *The War of the Rebellion . . . Official Records.* Series I, Vol. LI, pt. II, pp. 752-753; Vol. XXIX, pt. II, pp. 639-640.

forth greater energies, and to prevent our falling into greater disasters. Our people have only to be true and united, to bear manfully the misfortunes incident to war, and all will come right in the end.

I know how prone we are to censure and how ready to blame others for the non-fulfillment of our expectations. This is unbecoming in a generous people, and I grieve to see its expression. The general remedy for the want of success in a military commander is his removal. This is natural, and, in many instances, proper. For, no matter what may be the ability of the officer, if he loses the confidence of his troops disaster must sooner or later ensue.

I have been prompted by these reflections more than once since my return from Pennsylvania to propose to Your Excellency the propriety of selecting another commander for this army. I have seen and heard of expression of discontent in the public journals at the result of the expedition. I do not know how far this feeling extends in the army. My brother officers have been too kind to report it, and so far the troops have been too generous to exhibit it. It is fair, however, to suppose that it does exist, and success is so necessary to us that nothing should be risked to secure it. I therefore, in all sincerity, request Your Excellency to take measures to supply my place. I do this with the more earnestness because no one is more aware than myself of my inability for the duties of my position. I cannot even accomplish what I myself desire. How can I fulfill the expectations of others? In addition I sensibly feel the growing failure of my bodily strength. I have not yet recovered from the attack I experienced the past spring. I am becoming more and more incapable of exertion, and am thus prevented from making the personal examinations and giving the personal supervision to the operations in the field which I feel to be necessary. I am so dull that in making use of the eyes of others I am frequently misled. Everything, therefore, points to the advantages to be derived from a new commander, and I the more anxiously urge the matter upon Your Excellency from my belief that a younger and abler man than myself can readily be attained. I know that he will have as gallant and brave an army as ever existed to second his efforts, and it would be the happiest day of my life to see at its head a worthy leader—one that would accomplish more than I could perform and all that I have wished. I hope Your Excellency will attribute my request to the true reason, the desire to serve my country, and to do all in my power to insure the success of her righteous cause.

I have no complaints to make of any one but myself. I have received nothing but kindness from those above me, and the most considerate attention from my comrades and companions in arms. To Your Excellency I am specially indebted for uniform kindness and consideration. You have done everything in your power to aid me in the work committed to my charge, without omitting anything to promote the general welfare. I pray that your efforts may at length be crowned with success, and that you may long live to enjoy the thanks of a grateful people.

With sentiments of great esteem, I am, very respectfully and truly, yours,

R. E. LEE,
*General*

RICHMOND, VA., *August 11, 1863*

General R. E. LEE,
*Commanding Army of Northern Virginia:*

Yours of 8th instant has been received. I am glad that you concur so entirely with me as to the want of our country in this trying hour, and am happy to add that after the first depression consequent upon our disaster in the west, indications have appeared that our people will exhibit that fortitude which we agree in believing is alone needful to secure ultimate success.

It well became Sidney Johnston, when overwhelmed by a senseless clamor, to admit the rule that success is the test of merit; and yet there has been nothing which I have found to require a greater effort of patience than to bear the criticisms of the ignorant, who pronounce everything a failure which does not equal their expectations or desires, and can see no good result which is not in the line of their own imaginings. I admit the propriety of your conclusions, that an officer who loses the confidence of his troops should have his position changed, whatever may be his ability, but when I read the sentence I was not at all prepared for the application you were about to make. Expressions of discontent in the public journals furnish but little evidence of the sentiment of an army. I wish it were otherwise, even though all the abuse of myself should be accepted as the results of honest observation. I say I wish I could feel that the public journals were not generally partisan nor venal.

Were you capable of stooping to it, you could easily surround yourself with those who would fill the press with your laudations, and seek to exalt you for what you had not done, rather than detract from the achievements which will make you and your army the subject of history and object of the world's admiration for generations to come.

I am truly sorry to know that you still feel the effects of the illness you suffered last spring, and can readily understand the embarrassments you experience in using the eyes of others, having been so much accustomed to make your own reconnaissances. Practice will, however, do much to relieve that embarrassment, and the minute knowledge of the country which you have acquired will render you less dependent for topographical information.

But suppose, my dear friend, that I were to admit, with all their implications, the points which you present, where am I to find that new commander who is to possess the greater ability which you believe to be required? I do not doubt the readiness with which you would give way to one who could accomplish all that you have wished, and you will do me the justice to believe that if Providence should kindly offer such a person for our use, I would not hesitate to avail of his services.

My sight is not sufficiently penetrating to discover such hidden merit, if it exists, and I have but used to you the language of sober earnestness when I have impressed upon you the propriety of avoiding all unnecessary exposure to danger, because I felt our country could not bear to lose you. To ask me to substitute you by some one in my judgment more fit to command, or who would possess more of the confidence of the army, or of the reflecting men of the country, is to demand an impossibility.

It only remains for me to hope that you will take all possible care of yourself, that your health and strength may be entirely restored, and that the Lord will preserve you for the important duties devolved upon you in the struggle of our suffering country for the independence which we have engaged in war to maintain.

As ever, very respectfully and truly, yours,

JEFFERSON DAVIS

# — 39 —

# LEE FORESEES ULTIMATE DEFEAT,
## August 23, 1864*

*At the time that Lee wrote this sombre letter he had held off Grant in the wilderness, moved the army across the James, and held the iron lines at Fredericksburg. The greatest danger yet confronted him. It was that his army seemed to be melting away; at this very time, it has been asserted, there were enough deserters and draft dodgers in the back country of Carolina to have doubled the numerical strength of his forces.*

✓                    ✓                    ✓

HEADQUARTERS, ARMY OF NORTHERN VIRGINIA,
*August 23, 1864*

JAMES A. SEDDON, Secretary of War.

SIR:

The subject of recruiting the ranks of our army is growing in importance and has occupied much of my attention. Unless some measures can be devised to replace our losses, the consequences may be disastrous. I think that there must be more men in the country liable to military duty than the small number of recruits received would seem to indicate. It has been several months since the passage of the last conscript law, and a large number of able bodied men and officers are engaged in enforcing it. They should by this time, if they have not been remiss, have brought out most of the men liable to conscription, and should have no duty to perform, except to send to the army those who arrive at the legal age of service.

I recommend that the facts of the case be investigated, and that if the officers and men engaged in enrolling have finished their work, with the exception indicated, they be

* Clifford Dowdey, ed., *The Wartime Papers of R. E. Lee* (Boston, 1961), pp. 843-844.

returned to the army, where their presence is much needed. It is evidently inexpedient to keep a larger number out of service in order to get a smaller. I would also respectfully recommend that the list of detailed men be revised, and that all details of arms bearing men be revoked, except in cases of absolute necessity. I have myself seen numbers of men claiming to be detailed in different parts of the country who it seemed to me might well be in service. The corps are generally secured or beyond the necessity of further labor, and I hope some of the agricultural details may be revoked. Our numbers are daily decreasing, and the time has arrived in my opinion when no man should be excused from service, except for the purpose of doing work absolutely necessary for the support of the army. If we had here a few thousand men more to hold the stronger parts of our lines where an attack is least likely to be made, it would enable us to employ with good effect our veteran troops. Without some increase of our strength, I cannot see how we are to escape the natural military consequences of the enemy's numerical superiority.

> Very respectfully, your obt servt
> R. E. LEE
> *Genl*

# — 40 —

# GRANT'S ANACONDA STRATEGY, 1864*

*The term "anaconda"—like so many terms famous in history—was first applied in derision, to the grand strategy formulated by the hapless General Winfield Scott. This strategy, which recognized the elementary fact that the South could win by standing merely on the defensive*

* The Personal Memoirs of U. S. Grant (New York, 1886), Vol. II, pp. 127-132.

*and wearing down Northern will to fight and that North-
ern victory required the total subjugation of the South,
was fundamentally sound. Abandoned, perforce, by
Scott's successors, it was adopted by General Grant when,
in March, 1864, he was appointed to the command of all
the Union Armies. The anaconda strategy was successful.*

✔        ✔        ✔

. . . The Union armies were now divided into nineteen
departments, though four of them in the West had been
concentrated into a single military division. The Army
of the Potomac was a separate command and had no
territorial limits. There were thus seventeen distinct
commanders. Before this time these various armies had
acted separately and independently of each other, giving
the enemy an opportunity often of depleting one command, not pressed, to reinforce another more actively
engaged. I determined to stop this. To this end I regarded the Army of the Potomac as the centre, and all
west to Memphis along the line described as our position
at the time, and north of it, the right wing; the Army of
the James, under General Butler, as the left wing, and
all the troops south, as a force in rear of the enemy.
Some of these latter were occupying positions from
which they could not render service proportionate to
their numerical strength. All such were depleted to the
minimum necessary to hold their positions as a guard
against blockade runners; where they could not do this
their positions were abandoned altogether. In this way
ten thousand men were added to the Army of the James
from South Carolina alone, with General Gillmore in
command. It was not contemplated that General Gillmore
should leave his department; but as most of his troops
were taken, presumably for active service, he asked to
accompany them and was permitted to do so. Officers and
soldiers on furlough, of whom there were many thousands,
were ordered to their proper commands; concentration
was the order of the day, and to have it accomplished in
time to advance at the earliest moment the roads would
permit was the problem.

As a reinforcement to the Army of the Potomac, or to
act in support of it, the 9th army corps, over twenty
thousand strong, under General Burnside, had been
rendezvoused at Annapolis, Maryland. This was an ad-

mirable position for such a reinforcement. The corps could be brought at the last moment as a reinforcement to the Army of the Potomac, or it could be thrown on the sea-coast, south of Norfolk, in Virginia or North Carolina, to operate against Richmond from that direction. In fact Burnside and the War Department both thought the 9th corps was intended for such an expedition up to the last moment.

My general plan now was to concentrate all the force possible against the Confederate armies in the field. There were but two such, as we have seen, east of the Mississippi River and facing north. The Army of Northern Virginia, General Robert E. Lee commanding, was on the south bank of the Rapidan, confronting the Army of the Potomac; the second, under General Joseph E. Johnston, was at Dalton, Georgia, opposed to Sherman who was still at Chattanooga. Beside these main armies the Confederates had to guard the Shenandoah Valley, a great storehouse to feed their armies from, and their line of communications from Richmond to Tennessee. Forrest, a brave and intrepid cavalry general, was in the West with a large force; making a larger command necessary to hold what we had gained in Middle and West Tennessee. We could not abandon any territory north of the line held by the enemy because it would lay the Northern States open to invasion. But as the Army of the Potomac was the principal garrison for the protection of Washington even while it was moving on Lee, so all the forces to the west, and the Army of the James, guarded their special trusts when advancing from them as well as when remaining at them. Better indeed, for they forced the enemy to guard his own lines and resources at a greater distance from ours, and with a greater force. Little expeditions could not so well be sent out to destroy a bridge or tear up a few miles of railroad track, burn a storehouse, or inflict other little annoyances. Accordingly I arranged for a simultaneous movement all along the line. Sherman was to move from Chattanooga, Johnston's army and Atlanta being his objective points. Crook, commanding in West Virginia, was to move from the mouth of the Gauley River with a cavalry force and some artillery, the Virginia and Tennessee Railroad to be his objective. Either the enemy would have to keep a large force to protect their communications, or see them destroyed and a large amount of forage and provision, which they so much needed, fall into our hands. Sigel was in command in the Valley of Virginia. He was to advance up the valley, covering the North from an invasion through that channel as well while advancing as by remaining near Harper's Ferry. Every mile he advanced also gave us possession of stores on which Lee relied. Butler was to advance by the James River, having Richmond and Petersburg as his objective. . . .

— 41 —

# SECRETARY BENJAMIN RECALLS THE MISTAKES OF THE CONFEDERACY*

*The Confederate government was no more ready for war than was the Union government, and confusion and mismanagement attended the beginnings of that conflict on both sides. Even more serious than incompetence and shortsightedness, as events were to prove, was that jealousy between state and federal governments to which Secretary Benjamin here refers.*

*Benjamin was successively Attorney General, Secretary of War, and Secretary of State of the Confederacy, and probably the ablest and most trusted of President Davis's advisers. This letter was written after the war to Charles Marshall, an aide-de-camp of Lee.*

✓          ✓          ✓

As soon as war became certain, every possible effort was made by the President and his advisers to induce Congress to raise an army enlisted "for the war." The fatal effects of enlistments for short terms, shown by the history of the War of Independence against England,

* Sir Frederick Maurice, ed., *An Aide-de-Camp of Lee, Papers of Charles Marshall* (Boston, 1927), pp. 14-18.

were invoked as furnishing a lesson for our guidance. It was all in vain. The people as we were informed by the members would not volunteer for the war, but they would rise in mass as volunteers for twelve months. We did not wish them to rise in mass nor in great numbers for any such short term, for the reason that *we could not arm them,* and their term of service would expire before we could equip them. I speak from memory as to numbers, but only a moderate force was raised (all that we could provide with arms) for twelve months service, and thus a *provisional* army was formed, but the fatal effect of the short term of service, combined with the painful deficiency of supplies, were felt long before the end of the year. While the Northern States after the Battle of Manassas were vigorously engaged in preparing for an overwhelming descent upon Virginia, our own army was falling to pieces. . . .

The representatives of the people could not be persuaded to pass measures unpalatable to the people; and the unthinking multitude upon whose *voluntary* enlistments Congress forced us to depend were unable to foresee or appreciate the dangers of the policy against which we protested. It was only the imminent danger of being left without *any* army by the return home in mass of the first levy of twelve-month volunteers that drove Congress into passing a law for enlistments for the war, and in order to induce the soldiers under arms to re-enlist we were driven to the fatal expedient of granting them not only bounties but furloughs to return from Virginia to their homes in the far South, and if our actual condition had been at all suspected by the enemy they might have marched through Virginia with but the faintest show of resistance.

As to supplies of munitions I will give a single instance of the straits to which we were reduced. I was Secretary of War *ad interim* for a few months, during which Roanoke Island, commanded by General Wise, fell into the hands of the enemy. The report of that General shows that the capture was due in great measure to the persistent disregard by the Secretary of War of his urgent demands for munitions and supplies. Congress appointed a committee to investigate the conduct of the Secretary. I consulted the President whether it was best for the country that I should submit to unmerited censure or reveal to a

Congressional Committee our poverty and my utter inability to supply the requisitions of General Wise, and thus run the risk that the fact should become known to some of the spies of the enemy of whose activity we were well assured. It was thought best for the public service that I should suffer the blame in silence and a report of censure on me was accordingly made by the Committee of Congress.

The *dearth* even of powder was so great that during the descent of the enemy on Roanoke, General Wise having sent me a despatch that he was in instant need of ammunition, I ordered by telegraph General Huger at Norfolk to send an immediate supply; this was done but accompanied by a despatch from General Huger protesting against this exhausting of his small store, and saying that it was insufficient to defend Norfolk for a day. General Lee was therefore ordered to send a part of his very scanty supply to Norfolk, General Lee being in his turn aided by a small cargo of powder which had just run into one of the inlets on the coast of Florida.

Another terrible source of trouble, disorganisation and inefficiency was the incurable jealousy in many states of the General Government. Each State has its own mode of appointing officers, generally by election. Until disaster forced Congress to pass the Conscription law, all that we could do was to get laws passed calling for certain quotas of troops from the states, and in order to prevent attempts made to create officers of higher rank than the Confederate officers, who would thus have been placed under the orders of raw militia generals, we resorted to the expedient of refusing to receive any higher organisation than a regiment. But the troops being State troops officered by the State officers, the army was constantly scandalized by electioneering to replace regimental officers, and Confederate Commanders were without means of enforcing discipline and efficiency except through the cumbrous and most objectionable expedient of Courts Martial. Another fatal defect was that we had no power to consolidate regiments, battalions, and companies. If a company was reduced to five men or a regiment to fifty, we had no power to remedy this. The message of the President of the 12th of August, 1862, showed the fatal effects of our military system, and a perusal of that message will shed a flood of light on the actual position of things and the hopeless helplessness to which the Executive was reduced by the legislation of Congress, and the restrictions imposed on his power to act efficiently for military success by the jealousy of Congress and the States. When I look back on it all, I am lost in amazement that the struggle could have been so prolonged, and one of the main, if not the main strength and encouragement to the Executive was the genius, ability, constancy, fidelity, and firmness of General Lee.

# Part VI

# WARTIME RECONSTRUCTION

## — 42 —

## PROCLAMATION OF AMNESTY AND RECONSTRUCTION, December 8, 1863 *

*Lincoln, who adopted and consistently held the principle that the Union was indissoluble and secession illegal, saw from the beginning that the task of reconstruction was not that of punishing the rebellious South or of devising constitutional dialectic, but of getting the Southern states "into their proper practical relation with the rest of the Union." To this end, he began to formulate his reconstruction policies very early in the War. He had already indicated his reconstruction policy by his action during 1862 in the reconstruction of Tennessee and Louisiana. The Presidential plan, as presented in the message of December 8, 1863, provided for the restoration of loyal governments in the seceded states when a number, equal to one-tenth of the voting population of that state in 1860, should take a prescribed oath and organize a government. This Presidential plan assumed that the States were not out of the Union and that reconstruction was a Presidential function to be carried out through the instrumentality of the pardoning power. The opposition to this theory was announced first by the refusal of Congress to*

* Richardson, ed., *Messages and Papers of the Confederacy*, Vol. VI, pp. 213 ff.

*admit representatives from the reconstructed States and, decisively, by the passage of the Wade-Davis Bill.*

✓     ✓     ✓

*Whereas* in and by the Constitution of the United States it is provided that the President "shall have power to grant reprieves and pardons for offenses against the United States, except in cases of impeachment;" and

*Whereas* a rebellion now exists whereby the loyal State governments of several States have for a long time been subverted, and many persons have committed and are now guilty of treason against the United States; and

*Whereas,* with reference to said rebellion and treason, laws have been enacted by Congress declaring forfeitures and confiscation of property and liberation of slaves, all upon terms and conditions therein stated, and also declaring that the President was thereby authorized at any time thereafter, by proclamation, to extend to persons who may have participated in the existing rebellion in any State or part thereof pardon and amnesty, with such exceptions and at such times and on such conditions as he may deem expedient for the public welfare; and

*Whereas* the Congressional declaration for limited and conditional pardon accords with well-established judicial exposition of the pardoning power; and

*Whereas,* with reference to said rebellion, the President of the United States has issued several proclamations with provisions in regard to the liberation of slaves; and

*Whereas* it is now desired by some persons heretofore engaged in said rebellion to resume their allegiance to the United States and to reinaugurate loyal State governments within and for their respective States:

*Therefore,* I, Abraham Lincoln, President of the United States, do proclaim, . . . to all persons who have, directly or by implication, participated in the existing rebellion, except as hereinafter excepted, that a full pardon is hereby granted to them and each of them, with restoration of all rights of property, except as to slaves and in property cases where rights of third parties shall have intervened, and upon the condition that every such person shall take and subscribe an oath and thenceforward keep and maintain said oath inviolate, and which oath shall be registered for permanent preservation and shall be of the tenor and effect following, to wit:

I, —— ——, do solemnly swear, in presence of Almighty God, that I will henceforth faithfully support, protect, and defend the Constitution of the United States and the Union of the States thereunder; and that I will in like manner abide by and faithfully support all acts of Congress passed during the existing rebellion with reference to slaves, so long and so far as not repealed, modified, or held void by Congress or by decision of the Supreme Court; and that I will in like manner abide by and faithfully support all proclamations of the President made during the existing rebellion having reference to slaves, so long and so far as not modified or declared void by decision of the Supreme Court. So help me God.

The persons excepted from the benefits of the foregoing provisions are all who are or shall have been civil or diplomatic officers or agents of the so-called Confederate Government; all who have left judicial stations under the United States to aid the rebellion; all who are or shall have been military or naval officers of said so-called Confederate Government above the rank of colonel in the army or of lieutenant in the navy; all who left seats in the United States Congress to aid the rebellion; all who resigned commissions in the Army or Navy of the United States and afterwards aided the rebellion; and all who have engaged in any way in treating colored persons, or white persons in charge of such, otherwise than lawfully as prisoners of war, and which persons may have been found in the United States service as soldiers, seamen, or in any other capacity.

And I do further proclaim, declare, and make known that whenever, in any of the States of Arkansas, Texas, Louisiana, Mississippi, Tennessee, Alabama, Georgia, Florida, South Carolina, and North Carolina, a number of persons, not less than one-tenth in number of the votes cast in such State at the Presidential election of the year A. D. 1860, each having taken oath aforesaid, and not having since violated it, and being a qualified voter by the election law of the State existing immediately before the so-called act of secession, and excluding all others, shall re-establish a State government which shall be republican and in nowise contravening said oath, such shall be recognized as the true government of the State, and the State shall receive thereunder the benefits of the constitutional provision which declares that "the United States shall guarantee to every State in this Union a republican form of government and shall protect each of them against invasion, and, on application of the legislature, or the executive (when the legislature can not be convened), against domestic violence."

And I do further proclaim, declare, and make known that any provision which may be adopted by such State government in relation to the freed people of such State which shall recognize and declare their permanent freedom, provide for their education, and which may yet be consistent as a temporary arrangement with their present condition as a laboring, landless, and homeless class, will not be objected to by the National Executive.

And it is suggested as not improper that in constructing a loyal State government in any State the name of the State, the boundary, the subdivisions, the constitution, and the general code of laws as before the rebellion be maintained, subject only to the modifications made necessary by the conditions hereinbefore stated, and such others, if any, not contravening said conditions and which may be deemed expedient by those framing the new State government.

To avoid misunderstanding, it may be proper to say that this proclamation, so far as it relates to State governments, has no reference to States wherein loyal State governments have all the while been maintained. And for the same reason it may be proper to further say that whether members sent to Congress from any State shall be admitted to seats constitutionally rests exclusively with the respective Houses, and not to any extent with the Executive. And, still further, that this proclamation is intended to present the people of the States wherein the national authority has been suspended and loyal State governments have been subverted a mode in and by which the national authority and loyal State governments may be reestablished within said States or in any of them; and while the mode presented is the best the Executive can suggest, with his present impressions, it must not be understood that no other possible mode would be acceptable.

ABRAHAM LINCOLN.

# — 43 —

# CONGRESS VERSUS THE PRESIDENT

*Lincoln's humane and enlightened plan of reconstruction was almost bound to arouse Congressional opposition, in part, because it was so generous, and in even larger part, because it assumed that the Executive, not the Congress, would be in charge of reconstruction. Congressional hostility to the Presidential plan culminated in the passage by a close vote of the Wade-Davis Bill. Benjamin Wade was a radical Senator from Ohio; Henry Winter Davis of Maryland was chairman of the House Foreign Relations Committee and one of the most powerful of Lincoln's opponents. Lincoln pocket-vetoed the Wade-Davis Bill and after the adjournment of Congress he issued a proclamation giving reasons for refusing to accept the Congressional plan.*

*Lincoln's pocket veto of the Wade-Davis Bill and his statement of opposition to the Congressional plan of reconstruction provoked a vindictive attack on Lincoln and the Presidential policy by the sponsors of the bill, Benjamin Wade and Henry Winter Davis. The Manifesto was published in the New York* Tribune, *August 5, and shortly thereafter in the other leading papers of the country. Rarely, during a presidential election, have powerful party leaders attacked their presidential candidates more savagely. It is not without interest to note that while Lincoln was triumphantly re-elected, Davis was defeated.*

✓            ✓            ✓

## A. The Wade-Davis Bill, July 8, 1864*

*An Act to guarantee to certain States whose Governments have been usurped or overthrown a Republican Form of Government.*

* Richardson, ed., *Messages and Papers of the Confederacy*, Vol. VI, pp. 223 ff.

*Be it enacted,* That in the states declared in rebellion against the United States, the President shall, by and with the advice and consent of the Senate, appoint for each a provisional governor, . . . who shall be charged with the civil administration of such state until a state government therein shall be recognized as hereinafter provided.

SEC. 2. That so soon as the military resistance to the United States shall have been suppressed in any such state, and the people thereof shall have sufficiently returned to their obedience to the constitution and the laws of the United States, the provisional governor shall direct the marshal of the United States, as speedily as may be, to name a sufficient number of deputies, and to enroll all white male citizens of the United States, resident in the state in their respective counties, and to request each one to take the oath to support the constitution of the United States, and in his enrolment to designate those who take and those who refuse to take that oath, which rolls shall be forthwith returned to the provisional governor; and if the persons taking that oath shall amount to a majority of the persons enrolled in the state, he shall, by proclamation, invite the loyal people of the state to elect delegates to a convention charged to declare the will of the people of the state relative to the reëstablishment of a state government subject to, and in conformity with, the constitution of the United States.

SEC. 3. That the convention shall consist of as many members as both houses of the last constitutional state legislature, apportioned by the provisional governor among the counties, parishes, or districts of the state, in proportion to the white population, returned as electors, by the marshal, in compliance with the provisions of this act. The provisional governor shall, . . . provide an adequate force to keep the peace during the election.

SEC. 4. That the delegates shall be elected by the loyal white male citizens of the United States of the age of twenty-one years, and resident at the time in the county, parish, or district in which they shall offer to vote, and enrolled as aforesaid, or absent in the military service of the United States, and who shall take and subscribe the oath of allegiance to the United States in the form contained in the act of July 2, 1862; and all such citizens of the United States who are in the military service of the

United States shall vote at the headquarters of their respective commands, under such regulations as may be prescribed by the provisional governor for the taking and return of their votes; but no person who has held or exercised any office, civil or military, state or confederate, under the rebel usurpation, or who has voluntarily borne arms against the United States, shall vote, or be eligible to be elected as delegate, at such election.

SEC. 5. That the said commissioners, . . . shall hold the election in conformity with this act and, . . . shall proceed in the manner used in the state prior to the rebellion. . . .

SEC. 6. That the provisional governor shall, by proclamation, convene the delegates elected as aforesaid, at the capital of the state. . . .

SEC. 7. That the convention shall declare, on behalf of the people of the state, their submission to the constitution and laws of the United States, and shall adopt the following provisions, hereby prescribed by the United States in the execution of the constitutional duty to guarantee a republican form of government to every state, and incorporate them in the constitution of the state, that is to say:

First. No person who has held or exercised any office, civil or military, except offices merely ministerial, and military offices below the grade of colonel, state or confederate, under the usurping power, shall vote for or be a member of the legislature, or governor.

Second. Involuntary servitude is forever prohibited, and the freedom of all persons is guaranteed in said state.

Third. No debt, state or confederate, created by or under the sanction of the usurping power, shall be recognized or paid by the state.

SEC. 8. That when the convention shall have adopted those provisions, it shall proceed to reëstablish a republican form of government, and ordain a constitution containing those provisions, which, when adopted, the convention shall by ordinance provide for submitting to the people of the state. . . .

SEC. 12. That all persons held to involuntary servitude or labor in the states aforesaid are hereby emancipated and discharged therefrom, and they and their posterity shall be forever free. And if any such persons or their posterity shall be restrained of liberty, under pretence of any claim to such service or labor, the courts of the United States shall, on habeas corpus, discharge them.

Sec. 13. That if any person declared free by this act, or any law of the United States, or any proclamation of the President, be restrained of liberty, with intent to be held in or reduced to involuntary servitude or labor, the person convicted before a court of competent jurisdiction of such act shall be punished by fine of not less than fifteen hundred dollars, and be imprisoned not less than five nor more than twenty years.

Sec. 14. That every person who shall hereafter hold or exercise any office, civil or military, except offices merely ministerial, and military offices below the grade of colonel, in the rebel service, state or confederate, is hereby declared not to be a citizen of the United States.

## B. Lincoln's Proclamation on the Wade-Davis Bill, July 8, 1864*

By the President of the United States:

*A Proclamation.*

*Whereas* at the late session Congress passed a bill "to guarantee to certain States whose governments have been usurped or overthrown a republican form of government," a copy of which is hereunto annexed; and

*Whereas,* the said bill was presented to the President of the United States for his approval less than one hour before the *sine die* adjournment of said session, and was not signed by him; and

*Whereas* the said bill contains, among other things, a plan for restoring the States in rebellion to their proper practical relation in the Union, which plan expresses the sense of Congress upon that subject, and which plan it is now thought fit to lay before the people for their consideration:

Now, therefore, I, Abraham Lincoln, President of the United States, do proclaim, declare, and make known that while I am (as I was in December last, when, by proclamation, I propounded a plan for restoration) unprepared by a formal approval of this bill to be inflexibly committed to any single plan of restoration, and while I am also unprepared to declare that the free State con-

---

* Richardson, ed., *Messages and Papers of the Confederacy,* Vol. VI, p. 222.

stitutions and governments already adopted and installed in Arkansas and Louisiana shall be set aside and held for naught, thereby repelling and discouraging the loyal citizens who have set up the same as to further effort, or to declare a constitutional competency in Congress to abolish slavery in States, but am at the same time sincerely hoping and expecting that a constitutional amendment abolishing slavery throughout the nation may be adopted, nevertheless I am fully satisfied with the system for restoration contained in the bill as one very proper plan for the loyal people of any State choosing to adopt it, and that I am and at all times shall be prepared to give the Executive aid and assistance to any such people so soon as the military resistance to the United States shall have been suppressed in any such State and the people thereof shall have sufficiently returned to their obedience to the Constitution and the laws of the United States, in which cases military governors will be appointed with directions to proceed according to the bill. . . .

ABRAHAM LINCOLN.

## C. The Wade-Davis Manifesto, August 5, 1864*

We have read without surprise, but not without indignation, the Proclamation of the President of the 8th of July. . . .

The President, by preventing this bill from becoming a law, holds the electoral votes of the rebel States at the dictation of his personal ambition.

If those votes turn the balance in his favor, is it to be supposed that his competitor, defeated by such means, will acquiesce?

If the rebel majority assert their supremacy in those States, and send votes which elect an enemy of the Government, will we not repel his claims?

And is not that civil war for the Presidency inaugurated by the votes of rebel States?

Seriously impressed with these dangers, Congress, *"the proper constituted authority,"* formally declared that there are no State governments in the rebel States, and provided for their erection at a proper time; and both the Senate and the House of Representatives rejected the Senators and Representatives chosen under the authority

* E. McPherson, ed., *Political History of the Rebellion* (Washington, D. C., 1864), pp. 332 ff.

of what the President calls the free constitution and government of Arkansas.

The President's proclamation *"holds for naught"* this judgment, and discards the authority of the Supreme Court, and strides headlong toward the anarchy his proclamation of the 8th of December inaugurated.

If electors for President be allowed to be chosen in either of those States, a sinister light will be cast on the motives which induced the President to "hold for naught" the will of Congress rather than his government in Louisiana and Arkansas.

That judgment of Congress which the President defies was the exercise of an authority exclusively vested in Congress by the Constitution to determine what is the established government in a State, and in its own nature and by the highest judicial authority binding on all other departments of the Government. . . .

A more studied outrage on the legislative authority of the people has never been perpetrated.

Congress passed a bill; the President refused to approve it, and then by proclamation puts as much of it in force as he sees fit, and proposes to execute those parts by officers unknown to the laws of the United States and not subject to the confirmation of the Senate!

The bill directed the appointment of Provisional Governors by and with the advice and consent of the Senate.

The President, after defeating the law, proposes to appoint without law, and without the advice and consent of the Senate, *Military* Governors for the rebel States!

He has already exercised this dictatorial usurpation in Louisiana, and he defeated the bill to prevent its limitation. . . .

The President has greatly presumed on the forbearance which the supporters of his Administration have so long practiced, in view of the arduous conflict in which we are engaged, and the reckless ferocity of our political opponents.

But he must understand that our support is of a cause and not of a man; that the authority of Congress is paramount and must be respected; that the whole body of the Union men of Congress will not submit to be impeached by him of rash and unconstitutional legislation; and if he wishes our support, he must confine himself to his executive duties—to obey and execute, not make the laws—

to suppress by arms armed rebellion, and leave political reorganization to Congress.

If the supporters of the Government fail to insist on this, they become responsible for the usurpations which they fail to rebuke, and are justly liable to the indignation of the people whose rights and security, committed to their keeping, they sacrifice.

Let them consider the remedy for these usurpations, and, having found it, fearlessly execute it.

# — 44 —

# Lincoln: SECOND INAUGURAL ADDRESS, March 4, 1865*

*Lincoln's Second Inaugural Address needs neither introduction nor explanation. It is included because it restates with moving eloquence Lincoln's humane policy toward the South.*

✝          ✝          ✝

FELLOW-COUNTRYMEN:—At this second appearing to take the oath of the presidential office there is less occasion for an extended address than there was at the first. Then a statement somewhat in detail of a course to be pursued seemed fitting and proper. Now, at the expiration of four years, during which public declarations have been constantly called forth on every point and phase of the great contest which still absorbs the attention and engrosses the energies of the nation, little that is new could be presented. The progress of our arms, upon which all else chiefly depends, is as well known to the public as to myself, and it is, I trust, reasonably satisfactory and encouraging to all. With high hope for the future, no prediction in regard to it is ventured.

* Richardson, ed., *Messages and Papers of the Confederacy,* Vol. VI, pp. 276 ff.

On the occasion corresponding to this four years ago all thoughts were anxiously directed to an impending civil war. All dreaded it, all sought to avert it. While the inaugural address was being delivered from this place, devoted altogether to *saving* the Union without war, insurgent agents were in the city seeking to *destroy* it without war—seeking to dissolve the Union and divide effects by negotiation. Both parties deprecated war, but one of them would *make* war rather than let the nation survive, and the other would *accept* war rather than let it perish, and the war came.

One eighth of the whole population was colored slaves, not distributed generally over the Union, but localized in the southern part of it. These slaves constituted a peculiar and powerful interest. All knew that this interest was somehow the cause of the war. To strengthen, perpetuate, and extend this interest was the object for which the insurgents would rend the Union even by war, while the Government claimed no right to do more than to restrict the territorial enlargement of it. Neither party expected for the war the magnitude or the duration which it has already attained. Neither anticipated that the *cause* of the conflict might cease with or even before the conflict itself should cease. Each looked for an easier triumph, and a result less fundamental and astounding. Both read the same Bible and pray to the same God, and each invokes His aid against the other. It may seem strange that any men should dare to ask a just God's assistance in wringing their bread from the sweat of other men's faces, but let us judge not, that we be not judged. The prayers of both could not be answered. That of neither has been answered fully. The Almighty has His own purposes. "Woe unto the world because of offenses; for it must needs be that offenses come, but woe to that man by whom the offense cometh." If we shall suppose that American slavery is one of those offenses which, in the providence of God, must needs come, but which, having continued through His appointed time, He now wills to remove, and that He gives to both North and South this terrible war as the woe due to those by whom the offense came, shall we discern therein any departure from those divine attributes which the believers in a living God always ascribe to Him? Fondly do we hope, fervently do we pray, that this mighty scourge of war may speedily pass away. Yet, if

God wills that it continue until all the wealth piled by the bondsman's two hundred and fifty years of unrequited toil shall be sunk, and until every drop of blood drawn with the lash shall be paid by another drawn with the sword, as was said three thousand years ago, so still it must be said, "The judgments of the Lord are true and righteous altogether."

With malice toward none, with charity for all, with firmness in the right as God gives us to see the right, let us strive on to finish the work we are in, to bind up the nation's wounds, to care for him who shall have borne the battle and for his widow and his orphan, to do all which may achieve and cherish a just and lasting peace among ourselves and with all nations.

— 45 —

# Lincoln: LAST PUBLIC ADDRESS, April 11, 1865 *

*On the evening of April 11, a crowd celebrating the end of the War called at the executive mansion. Lincoln addressed them from the balcony on the question of reconciliation and reconstruction. At the Cabinet meeting of Friday, April 14, Lincoln again spoke of the problem of reconstruction. "If we were wise and discreet," he said, according to Secretary Welles, "we should re-animate the states and get their governments in successful operation, with order prevailing and the Union re-established, before Congress came together in December. . . . There were men in Congress who, if their motives were good were nevertheless impracticable, and who possessed feelings of hate and vindictiveness in which he did not sympathize and could not participate. He hoped there would be no persecution, no bloody work after the*

* The Writings of Abraham Lincoln, Constitutional ed., Vol. VII, pp. 362 ff.

*war was over. None need expect he would take any part in hanging or killing those men, even the worst of them."*

✓          ✓          ✓

FELLOW-CITIZENS:—We meet this evening not in sorrow, but in gladness of heart. The evacuation of Petersburg and Richmond, and the surrender of the principal insurgent army, give hope of a righteous and speedy peace, whose joyous expression cannot be restrained. In the midst of this, however, He from whom all blessings flow must not be forgotten.

A call for a national thanksgiving is being prepared, and will be duly promulgated. . . . By these recent successes, the reinauguration of the national authority—reconstruction—which has had a large share of thought from the first, is pressed much more closely upon our attention. It is fraught with great difficulty. Unlike a case of war between independent nations, *there is no authorized organ for us to treat with*—no one man has authority to give up the rebellion for any other man. We simply must begin with and mould from disorganized and discordant elements. Nor is it a small additional embarrassment that we, the loyal people, differ among ourselves as to the mode, manner, and measure of reconstruction. As a general rule, I abstain from reading the reports of attacks upon myself, wishing not to be provoked by that to which I cannot properly offer an answer. In spite of this precaution, however, it comes to my knowledge that I am much censured for some supposed agency in setting up and seeking to sustain the new State government of Louisiana. In this I have done just so much and no more than the public knows. In the Annual Message of December, 1863, and the accompanying proclamation, I presented a plan of reconstruction, as the phrase goes, which I promised, if adopted by any State, would be acceptable to and sustained by the Executive Government of the nation. I distinctly stated that this was not the only plan which might possibly be acceptable, and I also distinctly protested that the Executive claimed no right to say when or whether members should be admitted to seats in Congress from such States. This plan was in advance submitted to the then Cabinet, and approved by every member of it. One of them suggested that I should then and in that connection apply the Emancipation

Proclamation to the theretofore excepted parts of Virginia and Louisiana; that I should drop the suggestion about apprenticeship for freed people, and that I should omit the protest against my own power in regard to the admission of members of Congress. But even he approved every part and parcel of the plan which has since been employed or touched by the action of Louisiana. The new constitution of Louisiana, declaring emancipation for the whole State, practically applies the proclamation to the part previously excepted. It does not adopt apprenticeship for freed people, and is silent, as it could not well be otherwise, about the admission of members to Congress. So that, as it applied to Louisiana, every member of the Cabinet fully approved the plan. The message went to Congress, and I received many commendations of the plan, written and verbal, and not a single objection to it from any professed emancipationist came to my knowledge until after the news reached Washington that the people of Louisiana had begun to move in accordance with it. From about July, 1862, I had corresponded with different persons supposed to be interested in seeking a reconstruction of a State government for Louisiana. When the message of 1863, with the plan before mentioned, reached New Orleans, General Banks wrote me that he was confident that the people, with his military co-operation, would reconstruct substantially on that plan. I wrote to him and some of them to try it. They tried it, and the result is known. Such has been my only agency in setting up the Louisiana government. As to sustaining it my promise is out, as before stated. But, as bad promises are better broken than kept, I shall treat this as a bad promise and break it, whenever I shall be convinced that keeping it is adverse to the public interest; but I have not yet been so convinced. I have been shown a letter on this subject, supposed to be an able one, in which the writer expresses regret that my mind has not seemed to be definitely fixed upon the question whether the seceded States, so called, are in the Union or out of it. It would perhaps add astonishment to his regret were he to learn that since I have found professed Union men endeavoring to answer that question, I have purposely forborne any public expression upon it. As appears to me, that question has not been nor yet is a practically material one, and that any discussion of it, while it thus remains practically immaterial, could have no effect other than the mischievous one of dividing our friends. As yet, whatever it may become, that question is bad as the basis of a controversy, and good for nothing at all—a merely pernicious abstraction. We all agree that the seceded States, so called, are out of their proper practical relation with the Union, and that the sole object of the Government, civil and military, in regard to those States, is to again get them into their proper practical relation. I believe that it is not only possible, but in fact easier, to do this without deciding or even considering whether those States have ever been out of the Union, than with it. Finding themselves safely at home, it would be utterly immaterial whether they had been abroad. Let us all join in doing the acts necessary to restore the proper practical relations between these States and the Union, and each forever after innocently indulge his own opinion whether, in doing the acts he brought the States from without into the Union, or only gave them proper assistance, they never having been out of it. The amount of constituency, so to speak, on which Louisiana government rests, would be more satisfactory to all if it contained fifty thousand, or thirty thousand, or even twenty thousand, instead of twelve thousand, as it does. It is also unsatisfactory to some that the elective franchise is not given to the colored man. I would myself prefer that it were now conferred on the very intelligent, and on those who serve our cause as soldiers. Still, the question is not whether the Louisiana government, as it stands, is quite all that is desirable. The question is, Will it be wiser to take it as it is and help to improve it, or to reject and disperse? Can Louisiana be brought into proper practical relation with the Union sooner by sustaining or by discarding her new State government? Some twelve thousand voters in the heretofore Slave State of Louisiana have sworn allegiance to the Union, assumed to be the rightful political power of the State, held elections, organized a State government, adopted a Free State constitution, giving the benefit of public schools equally to black and white, and empowering the Legislature to confer the elective franchise upon the colored man. This Legislature has already voted to ratify the Constitutional Amendment recently passed by Congress, abolishing slavery throughout the nation. These twelve thousand persons are thus fully committed to the Union and to perpetuate freedom in the State—committed to the very things, and nearly all things, the nation wants—and they ask the nation's recognition and its assistance to make good this committal. Now, if we reject and spurn them, we do our utmost to disorganize and disperse them. We, in fact, say to the white man: You are worthless or worse; we will neither help you nor be helped by you. To the blacks we say: This cup of liberty which these, your old masters, held to your lips, we will dash from you, and leave you to the chances of gathering the spilled and scattered contents in some vague and undefined when, where, and how. If this course, discouraging and paralyzing both white and black, has any tendency to bring Louisiana into proper practical relations with the Union, I have so far been unable to perceive it. If, on the contrary, we recognize and sustain the new government of Louisiana, the converse of all this is made true. We encourage the hearts and nerve the arms of twelve thousand to adhere to their work, and argue for it, and proselyte for it, and fight for it, and feed it, and grow it, and ripen it to a complete success. The colored man, too, in seeing all united for him, is inspired with vigilance, and energy, and daring to the same end. Grant that he desires the elective franchise, will he not attain it sooner by saving the already advanced steps towards it, than by running backward over them? Concede that the new government of Louisiana is only to what it should be as the egg is to the fowl, we shall sooner have the fowl by hatching the egg than by smashing it. Again, if we reject Louisiana, we also reject one vote in favor of the proposed amendment to the National Constitution. To meet this proposition, it has been argued that no more than three fourths of those States which have not attempted secession are necessary to validly ratify the amendment. I do not commit myself against this, further than to say that such a ratification would be questionable, and sure to be persistently questioned, while a ratification by three fourths of all the States would be unquestioned and unquestionable. I repeat the question, Can Louisiana be brought into proper practical relation with the Union sooner by sustaining or by discarding her new State government? What has been said of Louisiana will apply to other States. And yet so great peculiarities pertain to each State, and such important and sudden changes

occur in the same State, and withal so new and unprece-
dented is the whole case, that no exclusive and inflexible
plan can safely be prescribed as to details and collaterals.
Such exclusive and inflexible plan would surely become
a new entanglement. Important principles may and must
be inflexible. In the present situation as the phrase goes,
it may be my duty to make some new announcement to
the people of the South. I am considering, and shall not
fail to act, when satisfied that action will be proper.

# Part VII

# APPOMATTOX AND THE END

## — 46 —

## Jefferson Davis: LAST MESSAGE TO THE PEOPLE OF THE CONFEDERACY, April 4, 1865 *

*On April 2, the Confederate government abandoned Richmond and fled to Danville; the following day Richmond fell. President Davis's last appeal to the Confederate people reveals a stubborn determination to continue the War but, in this decision in which he was not supported by Lee, he was overruled by the course of events.*

✓ ✓ ✓

DANVILLE, VA. April 4, 1865.

TO THE PEOPLE OF THE CONFEDERATE STATES OF AMERICA:

The General in Chief of our Army has found it necessary to make such movements of the troops as to uncover the capital and thus involve the withdrawal of the Government from the city of Richmond.

It would be unwise, even were it possible, to conceal the great moral as well as material injury to our cause that must result from the occupation of Richmond by the enemy. It is equally unwise and unworthy of us, as pa-

---

* Richardson, ed., *Messages and Papers of the Confederacy,* Vol. I, pp. 568 ff.

triots engaged in a most sacred cause, to allow our energies to falter, our spirits to grow faint, or our efforts to become relaxed under reverses, however calamitous. While it has been to us a source of national pride that for four years of unequaled warfare we have been able, in close proximity to the center of the enemy's power, to maintain the seat of our chosen Government free from the pollution of his presence; while the memories of the heroic dead who have freely given their lives to its defense must ever remain enshrined in our hearts; while the preservation of the capital, which is usually regarded as the evidence to mankind of separate national existence, was an object very dear to us, it is also true, and should not be forgotten, that the loss which we have suffered is not without compensation. For many months the largest and finest army of the Confederacy, under the command of a leader whose presence inspires equal confidence in the troops and the people, has been greatly trammeled by the necessity of keeping constant watch over the approaches to the capital, and has thus been forced to forego more than one opportunity for promising enterprise. The hopes and confidence of the enemy have been constantly excited by the belief that their possession of Richmond would be the signal for our submission to their rule, and relieve them from the burden of war, as their failing resources admonish them it must be abandoned if not speedily brought to a successful close. It is for us, my countrymen, to show by our bearing under reverses how wretched has been the self-deception of those who have believed us less able to endure misfortune with fortitude than to encounter danger with courage. We have now entered upon a new phase of a struggle the memory of which is to endure for all ages and to shed an increasing luster upon our country.

Relieved from the necessity of guarding cities and particular points, important but not vital to our defense, with an army free to move from point to point and strike in detail the detachments and garrisons of the enemy, operating on the interior of our own country, where supplies are more accessible, and where the foe will be far removed from his own base and cut off from all succor in case of reverse, nothing is now needed to render our triumph certain but the exhibition of our own unquenchable resolve. Let us but will it, and we are free; and who, in the light of the past, dare doubt your purpose in the future?

Animated by the confidence in your spirit and fortitude, which never yet has failed me, I announce to you, fellow-countrymen, that it is my purpose to maintain your cause with my whole heart and soul; that I will never consent to abandon to the enemy one foot of the soil of any one of the States of the Confederacy. . . . If by stress of numbers we should ever be compelled to a temporary withdrawal from her limits, or those of any other border State, again and again will we return, until the baffled and exhausted enemy shall abandon in despair his endless and impossible task of making slaves of a people resolved to be free.

Let us not, then, despond, my countrymen; but, relying on the never-failing mercies and protecting care of our God, let us meet the foe with fresh defiance, with unconquered and unconquerable hearts.

JEFF'N DAVIS

## — 47 —

## GENERAL LEE SURRENDERS

### A. The Surrender at Appomattox, April 10, 1865*

*As early as April 7, Grant had suggested to Lee the propriety of surrender in order to avoid further bloodshed. Lee was not yet ready to give up. But on April 9, when he found his sadly decimated army surrounded, he knew that the end had come. "There is nothing left for me to do but go and see General Grant," said Lee, "and I would rather die a thousand deaths." There was, of course, one desperate alternative: to disperse his army and wage a kind of guerrilla warfare in the mountains of Virginia. Lee was far too wise and too high-minded to*

* Sir Frederick Maurice, ed., *An Aide-de-Camp of Lee, Papers of Charles Marshall* (Boston, 1927), pp. 268-274.

*countenance such a course of action. On the afternoon of April 9, Lee rode Traveller to the McLean house in Appomattox Court House and accepted Grant's terms of surrender.*

*We give here Colonel Charles Marshall's account of the famous scene in the McLean house.*

✓          ✓          ✓

We struck up the hill towards Appomattox Court House. There was a man named McLean who used to live on the first battle field of Manassas, at a house about a mile from Manassas Junction. He did n't like the war, and having seen the first battle of Manassas, he thought he would get away where there would n't be any more fighting, so he moved down to Appomattox Court House. General Lee told me to go forward and find a house where he could meet General Grant, and of all people, whom should I meet but McLean. I rode up to him and said, "Can you show me a house where General Lee and General Grant can meet together?" He took me into a house that was all dilapidated and that had no furniture in it. I told him it would n't do.

Then he said, "Maybe my house will do!" He lived in a very comfortable house, and I told him I thought that would suit. I had taken the orderly along with me, and I sent him back to bring General Lee and Babcock, who were coming on behind. I went into the house and sat down, and after a while General Lee and Babcock came in. Colonel Babcock told his orderly that he was to meet General Grant, who was coming on the road, and turn him in when he came along. So General Lee, Babcock and myself sat down in McLean's parlour and talked in the most friendly and affable way.

In about half an hour we heard horses, and the first thing I knew General Grant walked into the room. There were with him General Sheridan, General Ord, Colonel Badeau, General Porter, Colonel Parker, and quite a number of other officers whose names I do not recall.

General Lee was standing at the end of the room opposite the door when General Grant walked in. General Grant had on a sack coat, a loose fatigue coat, but he had no side arms. He looked as though he had had a pretty hard time. He had been riding and his clothes were somewhat dusty and a little soiled. He walked up to General

Lee and Lee recognized him at once. He had known him in the Mexican war. General Grant greeted him in the most cordial manner, and talked about the weather and other things in a very friendly way. Then General Grant brought up his officers and introduced them to General Lee.

I remember that General Lee asked for General Lawrence Williams, of the Army of the Potomac. That very morning General Williams had sent word by somebody to General Lee that Custis Lee, who had been captured at Sailor Creek and was reported killed, was not hurt, and General Lee asked General Grant where General Williams was, and if he could not send for him to come and see him. General Grant sent somebody out for General Williams, and when he came, General Lee thanked him for having sent him word about the safety of his son.

After a very free talk General Lee said to General Grant: "General, I have come to meet you in accordance with my letter to you this morning, to treat about the surrender of my army, and I think the best way would be for you to put your terms in writing."

General Grant said: "Yes; I believe it will."

So a Colonel Parker, General Grant's Aide-de-Camp, brought a little table over from a corner of the room, and General Grant wrote the terms and conditions of surrender on what we call field note paper, that is, a paper that makes a copy at the same time as the note is written. After he had written it, he took it over to General Lee.

General Lee was sitting at the side of the room; he rose and went to meet General Grant to take that paper and read it over. When he came to the part in which only public property was to be surrendered, and the officers were to retain their side arms and personal baggage, General Lee said: "That will have a very happy effect."

General Lee then said to General Grant: "General, our cavalrymen furnish their own horses; they are not Government horses, some of them may be, but of course you will find them out—any property that is public property, you will ascertain that, but it is nearly all private property, and these men will want to plough ground and plant corn."

General Grant answered that as the terms were written, only the officers were permitted to take their private property, but almost immediately he added that he supposed that most of the men in the ranks were small farmers, and that the United States did not want their horses. He would give orders to allow every man who claimed to own a horse or mule to take the animal home.

General Lee having again said that this would have an excellent effect, once more looked over the letter, and being satisfied with it, told me to write a reply. . . .

I heard General Grant say this: "Sheridan, how many rations have you?"

General Sheridan said: "How many do you want?" and General Grant said, "General Lee has about a thousand or fifteen hundred of our people prisoners, and they are faring the same as his men, but he tells me his have n't anything. Can you send them some rations?"

"Yes," he answered. They had gotten some of our rations, having captured a train.

General Grant said: "How many can you send?" and he replied "Twenty-five thousand rations."

General Grant asked if that would be enough, and General Lee replied "Plenty; plenty; an abundance;" and General Grant said to Sheridan "Order your commissary to send to the Confederate Commissary twenty-five thousand rations for our men and his men."

After a while Colonel Parker got through with his copy of General Grant's letter and I sat down to write a reply. I began it in the usual way: "I have the honor to acknowledge the receipt of your letter of such a date," and then went on to say the terms were satisfactory.

I took the letter over to General Lee, and he read it and said: "Don't say, 'I have the honor to acknowledge the receipt of your letter of such a date'; he is here; just say, 'I accept these terms.'"

Then I wrote:—

HEADQUARTERS OF THE ARMY OF NORTHERN VIRGINIA,
April 9, 1865

I received your letter of this date containing the terms of the surrender of the Army of Northern Virginia proposed by you. As they are substantially the same as those expressed in your letter of the 8th instant, they are accepted. I will proceed to designate the proper officers to carry the stipulations into effect.

Then General Grant signed his letter, and I turned over my letter to General Lee and he signed it. Parker handed me General Grant's letter, and I handed him General Lee's reply, and the surrender was accomplished. There was no theatrical display about it. It was in itself perhaps the greatest tragedy that ever occurred in the history of the world, but it was the simplest, plainest, and most thoroughly devoid of any attempt at effect, that you can imagine.

The story of General Grant returning General Lee's sword to him is absurd, because General Grant proposed in his letter that the officers of the Confederate Army should retain their side-arms. Why, in the name of common sense, anybody should imagine that General Lee, after receiving a letter which said that he should retain his side-arms, yet should offer to surrender his sword to General Grant, is hard to understand. The only thing of the kind that occurred in the whole course of the transaction—which occupied perhaps an hour—was this: General Lee was in full uniform. He had on the handsomest uniform I ever saw him wear; and he had on a sword with a gold, a very handsome gold and leather, scabbard that had been presented to him by English ladies. General Grant excused himself to General Lee towards the close of the conversation between them, for not having his side arms with him; he told him that when he got his letter he was about four miles from his wagon in which his arms and uniform were, and he said that he had thought that General Lee would rather receive him as he was, than be detained, while he sent back to get his sword and uniform. General Lee told him he was very much obliged to him and was very glad indeed that he had n't done it.

## B. Lee Bids Farewell to the Army of Northern Virginia, April 10, 1865*

*This document needs no explanation. It is appropriate, however, to add a word about Lee after the War. Deeply convinced that the only hope for the South lay in a sincere acceptance of the verdict of Appomattox, he devoted himself to healing the wounds of war and training a generation of young men who might work for the reconstruction of their section. In June, 1865, he set an example to others by applying for a Presidential pardon;*

* Robert E. Lee, Jr., *Recollections and Letters of General Robert E. Lee* (New York, 1904), pp. 153-154.

*it is mortifying to record that the pardon was never granted. In September, 1865, Lee accepted the presidency of Washington College (now Washington and Lee University) at Lexington, Virginia, and as President inaugurated a series of interesting reforms in the direction of what we would now call progressive education. Stricken with angina pectoris, he died on October 12, 1870, and was buried in Lexington.*

*In Benét's fine phrase, Lee had "such glamour as can wear sheer triumph out"; if the cause for which he fought did not triumph, who can doubt that the admiration and affection in which he came to be held, by the North as well as the South, represented a triumph that has few parallels in history?*

✝        ✝        ✝

## HEADQUARTERS, ARMY OF NORTHERN VIRGINIA,
### April 10, 1865

After four years of arduous service, marked by un-unsurpassed courage and fortitude, the Army of Northern Virginia has been compelled to yield to overwhelming numbers and resources. I need not tell the survivors of so many hard-fought battles, who have remained steadfast to the last, that I have consented to this result from no distrust of them; but, feeling that valour and devotion could accomplish nothing that could compensate for the loss that would have attended the continuation of the contest, I have determined to avoid the useless sacrifice of those whose past services have endeared them to their countrymen. By the terms of the agreement, officers and men can return to their homes and remain there until exchanged. You will take with you the satisfaction that proceeds from the consciousness of duty faithfully performed; and I earnestly pray that a merciful God will extend to you His blessing and protection. With an increasing admiration of your constancy and devotion to your country, and a grateful remembrance of your kind and generous consideration of myself, I bid you an affectionate farewell.

R. E. LEE,
*General*

# — 48 —

# GENERAL JOHNSTON SURRENDERS, April 18, 1865 *

*The failure of Lee to escape from Grant and Sheridan and the surrender of the Army of Northern Virginia, April 9, left Johnston's army the only large Confederate force still in the field. The terms of Johnston's surrender to Sherman were on the general lines of those given to Lee by Grant and apparently had been outlined by Lincoln. These terms, however, were disapproved by Secretary of War Stanton, and Sherman was ordered to advance upon Johnston's army. Johnston agreed to new terms on April 26. Stanton's disapproval of Sherman's course of action led to a violent altercation between the two men, in which the Secretary of War appeared in a very unhappy light.*

✓          ✓          ✓

Memorandum between General Joseph E. Johnston and Major-General William T. Sherman, April 18, 1865

1. The contending armies now in the field to maintain the *status quo* until notice is given by the commanding general of any one to its opponent, and reasonable time —say, forty-eight hours—allowed.

2. The Confederate armies now in existence to be disbanded and conducted to their several State capitals, there to deposit their arms and public property in the State Arsenal; and each officer and man to execute and file an agreement to cease from acts of war, and to abide the action of the State an Federal authority. The number of arms and munitions of war to be reported to the Chief of Ordnance at Washington City, subject to the future action of the Congress of the United States, and, in the meantime, to be used solely to maintain peace and order within the borders of the States respectively.

* *Memoirs of General W. T. Sherman,* Vol. II, pp. 356-357.

3. The recognition, by the Executive of the United States, of the several State governments, on their officers and Legislatures taking the oaths prescribed by the Constitution of the United States, and, where conflicting State governments have resulted from the war, the legitimacy of all shall be submitted to the Supreme Court of the United States.

4. The reestablishment of all the Federal Courts in the several States, with powers as defined by the Constitution of the United States and of the States respectively.

5. The people and inhabitants of all the States to be guaranteed, so far as the Executive can, their political rights and franchises, as well as their rights of person and property, as defined by the Constitution of the United States and of the States respectively.

6. The Executive authority of the Government of the United States not to disturb any of the people by reason of the late war, so long as they live in peace and quiet, abstain from acts of armed hostility, and obey the laws in existence at the place of their residence.

7. In general terms—the war to cease; a general amnesty, so far as the Executive of the United States can command, on condition of the disbandment of the Confederate armies, the distribution of the arms, and the resumption of peaceful pursuits by the officers and men hitherto composing said armies.

— 49 —

# THE ASSASSINATION
## OF LINCOLN, April 14, 1865*

*Lincoln had gone to Richmond the day after the Confederates had evacuated it—calling, while there, on Mrs. Pickett—and then returned to Washington in time to make a memorable address on reconstruction. On the eve-*

* *Diary of Gideon Welles* (Boston, 1911), Vol. II, pp. 283 ff.

*ning of April 14, he went to Ford's Theater to see Laura
Keene in an English comedy,* Our American Cousin.
*John Wilkes Booth, brother of the more famous Edwin
Booth, had concocted a plot to assassinate all the principal officers of the government. John Booth, a Southern
sympathizer, was by now unbalanced. He thought that his
plan of assassination might undo the work of the Union
Armies and save the South. Entering Lincoln's box, he
sent a ball through the President's head, then leaped to
the stage, shouting, "Sic semper tyrannis!" Booth escaped
but was killed about two weeks later when he tried to
leave his hiding place, a Virginia barn.*

*The moving story of Lincoln's death is told by Navy
Secretary Gideon Welles.*

✓                  ✓                  ✓

I had retired to bed about half past-ten on the evening
of the 14th of April, and was just getting asleep when
Mrs. Welles, my wife, said some one was at our door.
Sitting up in bed, I heard a voice twice call to John, my
son, whose sleeping-room was on the second floor directly
over the front entrance. I arose at once and raised a win-
dow, when my messenger, James Smith, called to me that
Mr. Lincoln, the President, had been shot, and said Secretary Seward and his son, Assistant Secretary Frederick
Seward, were assassinated. James was much alarmed and
excited. I told him his story was very incoherent and im-
probable, that he was associating men who were not together and liable to attack at the same time. "Where," I
inquired, "was the President when shot?" James said he
was at Ford's Theatre on 10th Street. "Well," said I,
"Secretary Seward is an invalid in bed in his house yonder
on 15th Street." James said he had been there, stopped in
at the house to make inquiry before alarming me.

I immediately dressed myself, and, against the earnest
remonstrance and appeals of my wife, went directly to
Mr. Seward's, whose residence was on the east side of
the square, mine being on the north. James accompanied
me. As we were crossing 15th Street, I saw four or five
men in earnest consultation, standing under the lamp on
the corner by St. John's Church. Before I had got half
across the street, the lamp was suddenly extinguished and
the knot of persons rapidly dispersed. For a moment,
and but a moment I was disconcerted to find myself in

darkness, but recollecting that it was late and about time for the moon to rise, I proceeded on, not having lost five steps, merely making a pause without stopping. Hurrying forward into 15th Street, I found it pretty full of people, especially so near the residence of Secretary Seward, where there were many soldiers as well as citizens already gathered.

Entering the house, I found the lower hall and office full of persons, and among them most of the foreign legations, all anxiously inquiring what truth there was in the horrible rumors afloat. I replied that my object was to ascertain the facts. Proceeding through the hall to the stairs, I found one, and I think two, of the servants there holding the crowd in check. The servants were frightened and appeared relieved to see me. I hastily asked what truth there was in the story that an assassin or assassins had entered the house and assaulted the Secretary. They said it was true, and that Mr. Frederick was also badly injured. They wished me to go up, but no others. . . . As I entered, I met Miss Fanny Seward, with whom I exchanged a single word, and proceeded to the foot of the bed. Dr. Verdi and, I think, two others were there. The bed was saturated with blood. The Secretary was lying on his back, the upper part of his head covered by a cloth, which extended down over his eyes. His mouth was open, the lower jaw dropping down. I exchanged a few whispered words with Dr. V. Secretary Stanton, who came after but almost simultaneously with me, made inquiries in a louder tone till admonished by a word from one of the physicians. We almost immediately withdrew and went into the adjoining front room, where lay Frederick Seward. His eyes were open but he did not move them, nor a limb, nor did he speak. Doctor White, who was in attendance, told me he was unconscious and more dangerously injured than his father.

As we descended the stairs, I asked Stanton what he had heard in regard to the President that was reliable. He said the President was shot at Ford's Theatre, that he had seen a man who was present and witnessed the occurrence. I said I would go immediately to the White House. Stanton told me the President was not there but was at the theatre. "Then," said I, "let us go immediately there." . . .

The President had been carried across the street from

the theatre, to the house of a Mr. Peterson. We entered by ascending a flight of steps above the basement and passing through a long hall to the rear, where the President lay extended on a bed, breathing heavily. Several surgeons were present, at least six, I should think more. Among them I was glad to observe Dr. Hall, who, however, soon left. I inquired of Dr. H., as I entered, the true condition of the President. He replied the President was dead to all intents, although he might live three hours or perhaps longer.

The giant sufferer lay extended diagonally across the bed, which was not long enough for him. He had been stripped of his clothes. His large arms, which were occasionally exposed, were of a size which one would scarce have expected from his spare appearance. His slow, full respiration lifted the clothes with each breath that he took. His features were calm and striking. I had never seen them appear to better advantage than for the first hour, perhaps, that I was there. After that, his right eye began to swell and that part of his face became discolored.

Senator Sumner was there, I think, when I entered. If not he came in soon after, as did Speaker Colfax, Mr. Secretary McCulloch, and the other members of the Cabinet, with the exception of Mr. Seward. A double guard was stationed at the door and on the sidewalk, to repress the crowd, which was of course highly excited and anxious. The room was small and overcrowded. The surgeons and members of the Cabinet were as many as should have been in the room, but there were many more, and the hall and other rooms in the front or main house were full. One of these rooms was occupied by Mrs. Lincoln and her attendants, with Miss Harris. Mr. Dixon and Mrs. Kinney came to her about twelve o'clock. About once an hour Mrs. Lincoln would repair to the bedside of her dying husband and with lamentation and tears remain until overcome by emotion.

(April 15.) A door which opened upon a porch or gallery, and also the windows, were kept open for fresh air. The night was dark, cloudy, and damp, and about six it began to rain. I remained in the room until then without sitting or leaving it, when, there being a vacant chair which some one left at the foot of the bed, I occupied it for nearly two hours, listening to the heavy groans, and witnessing the wasting life of the good and great man who was expiring before me. . . .

A little before seven, I went into the room where the dying President was rapidly drawing near the closing moments. His wife soon after made her last visit to him. The death-struggle had begun. Robert, his son, stood with several others at the head of the bed. He bore himself well, but on two occasions gave way to overpowering grief and sobbed aloud, turning his head and leaning on the shoulder of Senator Sumner. The respiration of the President became suspended at intervals, and at last entirely ceased at twenty-two minutes past seven. . . .

I went after breakfast to the Executive Mansion. There was a cheerless cold rain and everything seemed gloomy. On the Avenue in front of the White House were several hundred colored people, mostly women and children, weeping and wailing their loss. This crowd did not appear to diminish through the whole of that cold, wet day; they seemed not to know what was to be their fate since their great benefactor was dead, and their hopeless grief affected me more than almost anything else, though strong and brave men wept when I met them.

— 50 —

## James Russell Lowell: "BOW DOWN, DEAR LAND, FOR THOU HAST FOUND RELEASE," 1865 *

*In July, 1865, Harvard College held commemoration services for Harvard men who had given their lives to the preservation of the Union. Altogether 138 Harvard men had been killed, or died, in the Union armies—and*

* James Russell Lowell, "Ode Recited at the Harvard Commemoration," July 31, 1865, in *Poems*.

*64 in the Confederate armies. James Russell Lowell, then a Professor at Harvard College, was called upon to write an appropriate ode. "The ode itself," he said later, "was an improvisation . . . the whole thing came out of me with a rush." It is, by common consent, the finest of Lowell's poems and, with Walt Whitman's "When Lilacs Last in the Dooryard Bloomed," the most noble and moving poem to come out of the Civil War.*

✦            ✦            ✦

## XI

Not in anger, not in pride,
Pure from passion's mixture rude
Ever to base earth allied,
But with far-heard gratitude,
Still with heart and voice renewed,
To heroes living and dear martyrs dead,
The strain should close that consecrates our brave.
Lift the heart and lift the head!
Lofty be its mood and grave,
Not without a martial ring,
Not without a prouder tread
And a peal of exultation:
Little right has he to sing
Through whose heart in such an hour
Beats no march of conscious power,
Sweeps no tumult of elation!
'Tis no Man we celebrate,
By his country's victories great,
A hero half, and half the whim of Fate,
But the pith and marrow of a Nation
Drawing force from all her men,
Highest, humblest, weakest, all,
For her time of need, and then
Pulsing it again through them,
Till the basest can no longer cower,
Feeling his soul spring up divinely tall,
Touched but in passing by her mantle-hem.
Come back, then, noble pride, for 't is her dower!
How could poet ever tower,
If his passions, hopes, and fears,
If his triumphs and his tears,
Kept not measure with his people?

Boom, cannon, boom to all the winds and waves!
Clash out, glad bells, from every rocking steeple!
Banners, advance with triumph, bend your staves!
      And from every mountain-peak
      Let beacon-fire to answering beacon speak,
      Katahdin tell Monadnock, Whiteface he,
And so leap on it light from sea to sea,
      Till the glad news be sent
      Across a kindling continent,
Making earth feel more firm and air breathe braver:
"Be proud! for she is saved, and all have helped to save
            her!
      She that lifts up the manhood of the poor,
      She of the open soul and open door,
      With room about her hearth for all mankind!
      The fire is dreadful in her eyes no more;
      From her bold front the helm she doth unbind,
      Sends all her handmaid armies back to spin,
      And bids her navies, that so lately hurled
      Their crashing battle, hold their thunders in,
      Swimming like birds of calm along the unharmful
            shore.
      No challenge sends she to the elder world,
      That looked askance and hated; a light scorn
      Plays o'er her mouth, as round her mighty knees
      She calls her children back, and waits the morn
Of nobler day, enthroned between her subject seas."

## XII

Bow down, dear Land, for thou hast found release!
      Thy God, in these distempered days,
      Hath taught thee the sure wisdom of His ways,
And through thine enemies hath wrought thy peace!
      Bow down in prayer and praise!
No poorest in thy borders but may now
Lift to the juster skies a man's enfranchised brow.
O Beautiful! my Country! ours once more!
Smoothing thy gold of war-dishevelled hair
O'er such sweet brows as never other wore,
      And letting thy set lips,
      Freed from wrath's pale eclipse,
The rosy edges of their smile lay bare,
What words divine of lover or of poet
Could tell our love and make thee know it,

Among the Nations bright beyond compare?
    What were our lives without thee?
    What all our lives to save thee?
    We reck not what we gave thee;
    We will not dare to doubt thee,
But ask whatever else, and we will dare!